A Cry Is Heard

My path to peace

JEAN VANIER

with François-Xavier Maigre

TWENTY-THIRD
PUBLICATIONS

twentythirdpublications.com

Originally published in France by
Bayard Éditions, 2017
18, rue Barbès, 92128 Montrouge

Translation: Anne Louise Mahoney
Cover image: Philip Coulter
Back cover image: Martin Gould

TWENTY-THIRD PUBLICATIONS
One Montauk Avenue, Suite 200
New London, CT 06320
(860) 437-3012 or (800) 321-0411
www.twentythirdpublications.com

ISBN: 978-1-62785-391-0
Library of Congress Control Number: 2018949165
Printed in Canada.

 A division of Bayard, Inc.

The truth will make you free.

The Gospel of John 8:32

Table of Contents

1. Praise for the Gift of Encounter.. **6**

2. A Hidden Presence... **11**

3. Roadblocks within Me **12**

4. Towards Greater Freedom **15**

5. A European Childhood: Living between
   Hope and Threats... **17**

6. The Call of the Sea **20**

7. Leaving Everything Behind…... **22**

8. I Find a Spiritual Father **26**

9. "Do You Want to Be Our Friend?" **28**

10. The Small Inner Voice: My Ariadne's Thread............................. **31**

11. I Had Found a Home... **33**

12. A Sign of the Covenant.. **36**

13. Strength and Perseverance **38**

14. Freedom to Grow.. **41**

15. An Open Spirituality **44**

16. A Free Electron **48**

17. The Gospel in India **51**

18. Community: A Place of Healing and Liberation......................... **55**

19. Authority through Listening **60**

20. When Faith Sets Our Hearts Free.. **63**

21. Communion beyond Words **67**

22. Joy Is Tested.. **71**

23. Living with Our Weaknesses **74**

24. Freedom Hidden in Those Who Are Oppressed **77**

25. From Generosity to Encounter **82**

26. The Truth Springs Forth from Below **85**

27. "I Am Happy!" **89**

28. She Watches over Me **91**

29. Drawn to a Holy Spring **93**

30. What I Owe to John Paul II **95**

31. The Fear that the Messenger Overshadows the Message... **98**

32. Saint John and the Gospel of Freedom **101**

33. The Evolution of Humanity: Towards Greater Unity **104**

34. The Mystery of the Person **110**

35. Working for a More Humane Society **112**

36. From Ireland to Palestine, a Path of Peace **114**

37. A Few *Fioretti* **117**

38. Fr. Joseph Wresinski, Apostle of Transformation **121**

39. Two Lights for My Path **123**

40. The Power of Mercy **125**

41. An Encounter and a Risk **129**

42. The Cry **132**

43. Heaven's Ark **135**

44. Walking in Weakness **137**

45. The Joy of a Presence **140**

46. At the End of the Road... A Time of Waiting
    and a Promise **142**

1

Praise for the Gift of Encounter

This book grew out of a sense of urgency.

In the face of the sad spectacle of divisions, fears, wars and inequalities that pervades our world, in the face of the depression and despair of so many young people, I dare to share with you a path of hope that was opened to me.

During my life, it has been people with an intellectual disability who gradually transformed me, freeing me from my fears, revealing to me my own humanity. After the terrorist attacks that have hit various countries recently, it seemed more important than ever to witness to the fellowship that is possible between people of different cultures, religions and histories. All is not lost. A path to unity, fellowship and peace is possible. The future depends on each one of us. Pope Francis has encouraged us since the beginning of his pontificate to encounter the poorest, the marginalized and all those who are different in some way. He invites us to let ourselves be evangelized by them, to receive their share of wisdom. The pope calls us to live a culture of encounter.

Encountering difference and working constantly to build bridges and not walls: this is the path of peace.

For more than 50 years, the most vulnerable in our L'Arche communities have taught me to accept my own weaknesses and limits. By their side, I understood that I must break free from my resistance, my bursts of pride, to become more free so I can love them better and let myself be loved. The pope consistently calls us to love all those who have been set aside, weakened by broken relationships, marginalized and oppressed: people who have no home, prisoners and others. I am also thinking of people who are homosexual, who, in a way, often live their difference as marginalization in a world that has trouble accepting them. At L'Arche, I understood that the suffering of people with a disability gradually made me one with the suffering of refugees and migrants fleeing wars in the hope of a life that is more human and more free. I am now 89 years old, and my strength is waning. But I dare to cry: Let us set ourselves free! Free of our fears that build walls between groups and people. Free of our dreams of power that make us dominate others. Free of our rivalries, our desires to win, that blind us. Free of our race for success, our unhealthy possessions and our desire for superiority, which prevent us from living fully the culture of encounter and from making room for a world of peace and unity. These words go against the spirit of competition that tends to rule our modern societies. Always higher, always ahead; this approach can trap us in elitist groups where we feel protected. The oppressed with whom I share daily life have taught me otherwise. And I am a witness: true happiness can be found in living this hectic race in reverse. The people I live with taught me the path of joyful wisdom. With them, I slowly learned to relinquish myself, to lower myself, to accept myself with my weaknesses, even though I have a long way to go to become like them.

*

In the twilight of my life, I wanted to try to trace a few stages of this inner liberation.

My words are those of a poor man, in a constant state of conversion, who wants to share his passion for living and his commitment. I often meet young people who work in various fields: social action, interfaith dialogue, renewal for our planet Earth, welcoming of the most vulnerable.... I admire their enthusiasm: it tells me that help is on the way. I would like, through these words, to encourage all those who work for peace by tearing down walls.

Such an endeavour, with the weariness that comes with age, was a challenge. My friendship with François-Xavier Maigre, a poet and writer, editor of the magazine *Panorama* where I publish a column once a month, meant we could work on it together, patiently and cooperatively. This book would not exist without him, and I wish to warmly thank him for his time. François-Xavier would have been my grandson's age, if I had had one, and he was able to find the words to help me pass the torch to new generations. These pages reveal a special alchemy between my thought, my experience and the poetic sensibility of a young writer. For several months, we met often at my house, in Trosly. We shared and talked a lot… François-Xavier discovered a little of the intimacy of our home, Val fleuri, by sitting at our always lively table. And that is how, week after week, this praise for the gift of encounter was born…

✳

Did you know that L'Arche started almost by chance? Deep down, I had this desire for a life of community with the poor, rooted in the Gospel. The spark was ignited more than 50 years ago, when our societies were open to all kinds of new things. At that time, I discovered the atmosphere of violence in institutions for people with an intellectual disability. In one of those institutions, I became friends with two men, and I invited them to come with me. We started living together, and we laughed a lot. We were happy. We spent our happiest times in the kitchen, around the table. So many unforgettable moments… Then L'Arche grew, so wonderfully, through the gentle hand of God. If I was the engine behind it, no one was more surprised than I. We were simply responding to an urgent need. Requests poured in; we tried to welcome them. Volunteers from around the world came to help us. Some found their vocation there. Although inspired by Christianity, L'Arche gradually began to welcome Hindus, Muslims, Jews, Buddhists. Today, it includes 140 communities in around 40 countries on five continents. Together, we started to discover unity on a human level. We witnessed the possibility of shared happiness, despite our cultural differences. What's more, we found that life with people with intellectual disabilities is a source of unexpected joy. Many of them reveal an immense, sensitive and loving heart. Our international community grew quickly.

Little by little, I was transformed as I discovered a new vision for our society. The success of L'Arche brought me honours that I sometimes accepted, to draw attention to the richness of the most fragile. Proclaiming a message of fellowship – that is what motivated me more and more noticeably. Thanks to L'Arche, we learned that living with people with a disability is a way to heal our hearts, which are so often closed, and to go out and meet all those who bear the disability of marginalization and oppression. Transformed by the weakest, we discover that together we can work for a transformation of our societies. The most fragile open us up to hope.

When the news is at times grim and discouraging, when selfishness, fear, insecurity, despair and hate close us in on ourselves, I thought it was important to bear witness to this hope, in a new light.

As though the healing of fears that paralyze our world and are the source of our violence, our rejection of the other, our closing in on ourselves, depended on each of our private liberations.

So many walls arise between us. So many protective mechanisms harden our consciences. I think we need little signs of hope to create new paths... Paths that lead to universal fellowship.

Here are a few.

In their own quiet way, they inspired my journey
and have given me insight over the years ...

2

A Hidden Presence

If there is any wisdom that I can never get enough of, it is that of Etty Hillesum. In her journal, this young Jewish woman, who died at Auschwitz, talks of the existence of a well hidden in the depths of her being. In this well, she writes, lives God: "*Sometimes I am there too. But more often stones and grit block the well, and God is buried beneath. Then he must be dug out again.*"

To be in relationship with God, we must free ourselves of everything that prevents us from encountering him. I truly believe this. God is this hidden presence, this spring that can quench our thirst. We must go down to find him.

All it took for me to experience it was to let myself be led by the weakest, the most foolish and the most oppressed of our societies. A long road lay before me. I had to patiently learn to remove these stones, this rubble that prevented me from encountering God. And I am far from being finished. L'Arche allowed me to discover how much the walls that separate people can seem difficult to knock down, reinforced by the stones that lodge deep in our hearts and block the spring. It's all about how to remove them.

3

Roadblocks within Me

When I went to Chile a few years ago, Denis met me at the airport. He had offered to drive me to Santiago, a city of five million people, where I was going to visit our Faith and Light communities. There we were on the road. The first few kilometres passed under an enormous sun. My gaze was focused on the curving landscape when, at the side of the road, a pile of tin and cinderblocks appeared. Poverty in its rawest expression. This was only the first of the surprises awaiting me. On the other side of the road, just a few dozen metres away, the ambiance was very different. Luxury, calm, opulence. A striking contrast! Denis pulled over and told me a bit more.

"On the left are the slums of Santiago. On the right are the homes of rich families, under tight police and military protection." My host became silent. He looked at me sadly: "This road, Jean – no one ever crosses it." The rich are afraid of the poor, and the poor are afraid of the rich. Something powerful separates them. Like a wall. A border. Each group is locked behind its security walls. We are living in a paradox where some roads, designed to allow for communication, mark boundaries that cannot be crossed. But there are other barriers, more underground, that enclose our hearts. They are hidden from view. They feed on our most secret fears, our deepest wounds. They dry up our lives, without our realizing it. Experience has taught me that it is essential to topple them to experience true freedom, which our humanity is founded on and for which God made us.

Yes, the secret of a happy life may be tied to this process of liberation to lead us toward an inner spring that leads to universal fellowship. And the story of L'Arche is, in my eyes, a long and wonderful story of liberation. Gradually knocking down the walls that hide this spring, because we are afraid of our vulnerability. It prevents us from encountering the other who is different from us, loving them as God loves them. It's a daily struggle. At the beginning, every human person is born vulnerable, with their primal innocence. Look at the infant: it needs its mother and father to feel at peace, to feel secure, to know it is loved unconditionally. As the child grows up, they confront the world. They learn to do things for themselves, as if they have to prove they are loveable and capable. Their parents try to teach them as best they can, by loving them and protecting them. But whatever they do, this feeling of vulnerability never really disappears: it lurks in the deepest part of their being. Without always being aware of it, we move on with our original fragility. Unconsciously, it inspires our endless quests for power, our race for success, our need for recognition and our desire to own things. But, deep within ourselves, we thirst for the truly infinite. Love that would fill our whole being. Love that would heal our hurts. Love that would quench our thirst for relationship. And often, reality does not seem to meet our expectations. That is how, through disappointments and trials, we come to build impenetrable walls around our vulnerable hearts, but also around the groups we belong to. Through our defensive stance, we think we are protecting ourselves. In reality, these attitudes end up imprisoning us.

How can we break down our walls? First, by agreeing to name them. Words open up a powerful pathway for healing. Then, in discovering a new strength within ourselves, strength that can calm us and reassure us beyond all our hopes. The daily encounter with people who are weak allowed my barriers to gradually crack. I understood that true freedom involves approaching God through the presence and sacrament of the poor, as Saint John Chrysostom said. This life allowed me to grasp the promise of Jesus: "The truth will make you free."

4

Towards Greater Freedom

When I reflect on my own inner life, on my human and spiritual growth, I realize that the constant search for human achievement, for a kind of fullness, was at times my driving force.

Years later, something new drove me. I am always motivated by a greater desire to live with Jesus. It seems that my spiritual life deepened as the barriers around my heart crumbled. The more these buttresses fell, the more my true "me" sprang up. My inner self began to awaken. I found that I was vulnerable without being afraid. I felt my freedom awaken.

For me, this happened gradually. Day after day, season after season. Gently, I would even say. Almost unconsciously. I was tenderly led by the hand by the poor and the weak towards something ever new. As if I were slowly being stripped of my certainties, of all those desires, all those postures that were walling me in. As if I felt the urgent need to be set free from these desires for recognition, for domination. They did not always lead me to just relationships with certain people or to appropriate behaviours as the person in charge. I also am vulnerable; I long for relationship. At my age, I see clearly how these desires, which seem legitimate, are all driven by grasping tendencies, towards myself as well as towards others.

These gaps allowed me to move towards another desire, a peaceful but increasingly burning one. A desire for greater unity within me, and for peacemaking. A desire for unity around me, among people of different religions and cultures, and different abilities. For peace. Of course, I am still far from this total freedom that the Holy Spirit would like to give me. There are still, I am sure, many protective mechanisms that separate me from others and that need to come down – remaining anxieties, and buried fears whose causes and remedies I don't know. The future also holds difficult times for me, no doubt. Suffering, perhaps, when I myself become someone with a major disability. I am getting old and my strength is fading. That is a fact I cannot ignore.

Still, I am convinced that the challenges to come will lead me to a greater inner peace. A new happiness will be given to me in my old age. I hope to live this happiness in my final weakness – that is, when I die – welcomed in the tender arms of God, who will come to find me and fulfill me like a beloved friend.

5

A European Childhood:
Living between Hope and Threats

Let's go back in time... As far back as my memories go, nothing prepared me for such a life. It all began in my childhood, at the dawn of the 20th century's major ruptures. My parents, Georges and Pauline Vanier, originally from Quebec, were both deeply Christian. In 1938, during a sermon preached by an eloquent Jesuit, my father experienced a loving God for the first time – the intensity of a presence that suddenly enfolded his prayer in unexpected warmth. He who had been raised in the spirit of Jansenism, a rigid and austere approach, discovered faith in a new light. My mother came across as an exuberant, slightly depressive woman, but she had a great thirst for God. She became friends with several Carmelites, to whom she felt spiritually close.

This devotion shone through our family. There were five of us children: the eldest, my sister, Thérèse, who would become a palliative care physician and founder of L'Arche in the United Kingdom; my brother Benedict, who would join the Cistercian order; then Bernard, a little older than me, a future painter. I was the fourth. A younger brother, Michel, a wonderful man, would complete our ranks. Next to my older siblings, all very bright, I paled in comparison. I was seen as a mediocre student with little promise. To top it all off, my health was delicate. Thérèse and Benedict, who succeeded at everything, seemed out of reach at times. I was, however, close to Bernard, one year my senior, who played the role of protector. He was a good man. He watched over me.

✳

I was born in 1928, in Geneva, where my father was a military adviser with the League of Nations. He had taken up a diplomatic career after the painful and tragic period of the First World War. Papa had lost his right leg during a deadly attack in Pas-de-Calais at Chérisy in 1918, as part of Canada's famous 22nd Battalion (the Van Doos), of which he was a founding officer. Even before I was born, serious physical disability had entered our family history. Those three years in the mud of the trenches made my father an extraordinarily brave man. That inner strength shone in his face and affected those around him. In the infantry, under fire and amid falling bombs, he developed a keen sense of friendship. And he never forgot it. Even in 1931, when he became Secretary to the Office of the High Commissioner in the UK, my father knew how to stay faithful to who he was. In London, I had a happy childhood. We were taught by the Jesuits. But once again, we were to cross the Channel and move. At the beginning of 1939, Papa was appointed Minister Plenipotentiary of Canada in France. Suddenly, the war erupted, shaking up our lives and our plans. Caught up in this turmoil, we decided to stay together. We were refugees in a château in Sarthe that was requisitioned by the French government. In May 1940, German troops invaded France, by way of Belgium. I have clear memories of this time. I remember being part of this great exodus. My family and

I joined the French people in the exodus. After many twists and turns, we were able to flee towards Bordeaux. By taking a British Navy destroyer, and then a merchant marine ship, we were able to return, *in extremis*, to the UK.

A few months later, we went back to Canada, where as of 1941 my father was commander of the military district of Quebec. In Montreal, I was able to pick up my youth again, between the Jesuit school and Sundays spent as a family, always nourished by this rootedness in hope and in faith. In 1959, Papa became the governor general of Canada, the Queen of England's representative. He served in that role until his death. Although he held the nation's highest positions, he would remain such a humble man…

6

The Call of the Sea

I'll never forget that day. It was 1942. In our intellectual and military circle, the seriousness of the times left no one unmoved. We could not forget what we had lived in France. Worrisome news arrived each day from Europe, and, at the venerable age of 13, I felt a compelling desire rising in me: I wanted to enter the Royal Navy college in Dartmouth, England, which trained future Navy officers. Why? I have no idea. Was it to gain my independence? Was it the example of my own father, who was in the Canadian Army, that inspired this impulse? Was it a desire to work for peace in a world at war? I didn't know. It took hold of me and I couldn't fight it. It was a small inner voice that pushed me, and I couldn't resist it. I knew I had to go. Right away! But it wasn't that simple. Given my age, I needed my father's permission. He had just been made major general; I respected him as much as I was impressed by him. We found ourselves in his military office, Papa and me. Our discussion was amazing. After using some wonderful arguments to try to talk me out of going, my father, good general that he was, agreed to lower his guard. He understood. He didn't want to clip my wings. His response, filled with tenderness, still echoes in me: "I have confidence in you, as you know. If it's really what you want, then do it." What happened? The father believed in his son. And in doing so, he supported my deepest desire. In a way, he gave me a new freedom. He believed in me and my desires. He confirmed that I could have confidence in myself and in my small inner voice.

*

In May 1942, my father took me by train to the military port in Halifax, east of Montreal, where I sailed for England. There I was, an inexperienced young recruit, on a ship taking troops to European shores on the other side of the Atlantic. Our fleet included about 20 vessels, escorted by several destroyers. The crossing would be perilous; no one had any illusions about that. One boat in five was sunk by German submarines… Without further ado, I left my family – for the first time – leaving behind at the wharf a happy childhood and beloved faces… I left without knowing where the currents would take me.

This abrupt change, this deep and instantaneous loss of all the forms of security I had ever known, marked the beginning of a radically new life at the tender age of 13. I made this choice freely; against my parents' wishes, yes, but with their blessing. It was a leap into the unknown – a real one. Where did I get the strength that propelled me across the Atlantic towards England… and resulted in the founding of L'Arche 22 years later?

In England, I had to learn to live with insecurity, with the alarms and air raids. Ironically, the precariousness of this life, the ever-present danger, gave me a sense of security that I had never known before. I knew that I was free to choose. I discovered within me, in the heart of a Europe at war, a new strength. And little by little, I was able to befriend that confidence that grew silently within me.

7

Leaving Everything Behind...

Eight years in the Navy leaves its mark. I remember well the officers' school in Dartmouth, where I was a student for four years. My friends and I all wore the uniform proudly and couldn't wait to go to war on the ships. I spent my adolescence wanting to do missions in a tragic world. Like the rest of my generation, I was devastated when I found out what had happened at Auschwitz, that death factory and hell on earth, and learned of all the horror of the concentration camps in Germany. I see the Shoah as a permanent wound of humanity. I also have a clear memory of Japan's surrender in August 1945, following the dropping of two atomic bombs on Hiroshima and Nagasaki. For me, this was a moral conflict: human beings were able to kill each other on a scale never seen before. Nuclear weapons carried the risk of causing catastrophes threatening the survival of humanity. Then, in March 1946, Winston Churchill spoke, with his customary clear-headedness, of the iron curtain falling on Eastern Europe. And how could we overlook the "gulag Archipelago"? Alexander Solzhenitsyn later strongly denounced the scope of the repressive Soviet prison system that had existed since the October revolution. These horrors were the backdrop of my youth, even though I didn't experience them directly. I recognized the dangers of tyrannies that were developing at the expense of human beings, along with new weapons to serve their cause. But already, new perils were smouldering in the ashes of our past battles. The time of the Cold War did not bode well. On our ships, we prepared for more conflicts to come. How could we not feel great anxiety, a giddy awareness, in the face of the real risk of the start of a nuclear holocaust? A few years later, I welcomed seriously the healthy cry of Good Pope John, whom I knew a little, in his 1963 encyclical *Pacem in terris* (Peace on earth).

Despite the darkness of these days, I enjoyed my time in the Navy. I learned so much on the deck of a ship, starting with the valuable discipline of body and mind. I became a stronger person, encouraged by my superiors, who appreciated my dedication and prompted me to give the best of myself. Their attention helped me to grow up. A career as an officer awaited me. But as time passed, I felt drawn to something different. Prayer spoke to me. When I could, I went to mass. An amusing anecdote: in 1950, when I was sailing on the *Magnificent* – the only Canadian aircraft carrier – we anchored in the port of Havana, Cuba. We were given permission to go ashore. While all my officer friends got dressed up to go dancing in town, I parted company with them in the hope of finding a church. For them, the exhilaration of island pleasures; for me, the silence of a refuge where I could pray. I felt more and more drawn by Jesus, to the point of considering giving him my life. My whole life. The Navy was my second family. But at the same time, I felt a nagging anxiety. It didn't pass. I don't know what could have caused this feeling. Maybe I was lacking that rough and ready character that makes you a real sailor... After a while, it all became clear. I had to go. Deep within me, my small inner voice said, "Follow me." Follow me to better live the Gospel. Follow me to find the kingdom of God, the kingdom of Love. Work for peace – not with weapons of war, but as a disciple of Jesus.

Leaving everything behind, once again. Leaving… not to run away, but to be myself.

*

In the beginning, I thought about joining a small community of lay Catholics in Harlem, a turbulent black neighbourhood in New York. I had met them when the *Magnificent*, returning from Havana, moored in that famous US city. I felt deeply called by this community that I had visited several times. I felt that each of these lay people wanted to follow the example of Jesus, being poor among the poor. However, the Jesuit who accompanied me suggested that I take some time to give shape to my commitment, without rushing. So what to do? I wrote to three priests in confidence, men I knew or who had been recommended to me, sharing with them my desire to find a place to live for a year, to give me time to clarify my choices. Fr. Thomas Philippe, a Dominican, was the first to write back, inviting me to come to L'Eau Vive, an international lay centre for teaching theology that he had founded two years earlier in Soisy-sur-Seine, not far from Paris.

Without hesitation, I left the port of Halifax – the same one I had left for Europe eight years earlier – but this time it was on an ocean liner and without a military uniform. One civilian among others, for the first time in a long time. Breathing in the sea air, I bade farewell to the Nova Scotia coast that vanished in the fog along with my dreams of being a naval officer. I felt lighter. I looked forward to seeing my parents, who since September 1944 had been living in Paris, where my father had been named ambassador.

*

After a brief stopover with my family, I dropped anchor at L'Eau Vive, where Fr. Thomas was expecting me. I found a radically new world there, one far from the atmosphere of a ship. There I sought to live the Gospel in the simplicity and poverty of a community. Free to pray, to meditate. I was eager to discover the future place where I could serve Jesus for the rest of my life. I had given up the security of a military career and the comfortable salary that went with it. But I felt great joy. I had total confidence in God; I felt free. I had decided to follow what my heart and my small inner voice were telling me. Though I still didn't know where or how my spiritual plans were going, I had the strong feeling that I would become a priest.

8

I Find a Spiritual Father

At L'Eau Vive, I took part in the offices and the Eucharist every day. I learned Latin and was soon able to decipher it with ease. Two other disciplines enhanced my study of the humanities: I studied philosophy and theology at Saulchoir, the Dominican house of studies near Soisy. As I mentioned, I thought I would become a priest. Was that truly my vocation? I needed to know for sure. In 1951, I spent ten days with the Carthusians of La Valsainte in Switzerland, where I quickly realized that I was not suited to monastic life. I did not feel completely at home.

That is when I had a genuine encounter with Jesus in prayer for the first time. Until this point, I had always needed to fill myself up with words, with readings, to enter into prayer. I prayed the rosary. I meditated on the pages of the breviary. Now my prayer turned into a heart-to-heart with the invisible. It became a peaceful silence, a joy: the place where God was. I discovered that I was loved by Jesus. My spiritual life changed dramatically.

In that private space, I felt more and more drawn to Fr. Thomas, like a student to a teacher. Also like a young person seeking someone to show him the path of Jesus. I experienced significant and profound graces through prayer, in total abandon. My future would not be with the Carthusians or in another religious order. I sensed it would, however, be related to this Fr. Thomas, who was the only one to write back to me and whom I was getting to know. This process gave rise to a new insecurity: it was not up to me to decide on my future. It was God, through that small inner voice, who allowed me to discover, little by little, what he wanted for me. As my relationship with Fr. Thomas grew stronger, an unknown fullness filled me. I experienced intense joy and great freedom. I had found a spiritual father who trusted me completely. It was he who began to form my spiritual and theological intelligence, helping me to discover the conscience of the heart, the search for communion as the foundation of the human person and their growth in God's love. He also taught me about the filial relationship with Mary, the Mother of Jesus, who opens for us a path to her. This relationship with Fr. Thomas, who nurtured my emerging spiritual experience, was drastically shaken 50 years later, when I learned that he had abused a number of women within the context of spiritual direction. I will say more about this later.

9

"Do You Want to Be Our Friend?"

I spent two years at L'Eau Vive. In 1952, Fr. Thomas suddenly told us he was leaving, as his superiors had called him back to Rome. He hoped I would succeed him as leader of the community. The board of directors confirmed my appointment. But I felt ill equipped to take on such a responsibility – on a human, theological or spiritual level. At the same time, I trusted in God. I knew he would show me what I had to do. So I agreed. For a few years, I tried to maintain L'Eau Vive, faithful to the insights of Fr. Thomas – until that day in 1956 when the bishop of Versailles and the Dominican provincial asked me, on behalf of the Holy Office of Rome, to leave the community. "We'll give you three weeks," they told me. I later learned that Fr. Thomas had been disciplined by the leadership, but I did not know the real reasons for this decision, among the conflicting rumours that were circulating.

Once more, I was on my way, not knowing where to go. Thrust into the unknown. I did not intend to go and live with my parents, who had since returned to Canada. I had envisioned joining the Quebec seminary and then, once I was ordained, returning to serve at L'Eau Vive, and this plan had started to take shape. But I had to give it up. I suspected that I would not become a priest. In the meantime, I had to manage. I trusted in the Holy Spirit who would guide me. I would find a pathway that would allow me to live with Jesus, dedicated to him like the "eunuchs for the kingdom," as the Gospel of Saint Matthew (19:12) puts it. I was also sure I would one day meet up with Fr. Thomas again. He was my spiritual father.

I heard about a Cistercian monastery near Cholet, in France. Father Abbot invited me to stay for as long as I needed. I stayed for a year. In this atmosphere of prayer, the same question constantly came back to me: "Where am I called to build my life as a man and a disciple of Jesus?" After leaving the Trappist brothers to work on my doctorate in philosophy at the Institut catholique de Paris, I rented a small farm in Orne, in the countryside of Normandy. There I led a prayerful solitary existence.

Dwelling in this thirst for silence, I decided to surrender myself, once again, to divine Providence and a call from the Holy Spirit. My trip took me to Fatima, where the Virgin had appeared to three young peasants in 1917. In the middle of the Portuguese countryside, the peaceful Marian shrine opened its arms to me. There, far from all distraction, I finished my thesis on Aristotle's ethics. I loved this life of retreat, interiority and work. For a while, I could have been taken for a hermit. But I still didn't know where I would end up. An intuition (the small inner voice?) came to me in prayer: something will emerge. I waited confidently for a sign from God. Waiting, abandonment; a simple life. And a happy one.

*

In September 1962, after obtaining my doctorate in philosophy, an unexpected request came from Canada. I was invited to teach ethics at the University of Toronto. I joyfully accepted. From January to April 1964, I found it incredibly satisfying to share my passion with students. They listened to me with great interest, and I became fond of all these young people. No one was more surprised than I at the success of my classes. I would never have believed I had the slightest gift for teaching.

Thousands of kilometres away, shortly before Christmas 1963, Fr. Thomas became chaplain of Val fleuri, a centre created in Trosly-Breuil, in northern France, by a father for his son with a disability and others who were in the same situation. Dr. Préaut, an eminent local psychiatrist, oversaw this new kind of structure. Once my lectures were done, I returned to France, where I took the time to track down Fr. Thomas, for longer than our last meeting. But what a shock! Thanks to this time in Val, I discovered in a special way the world of people with an intellectual disability. Their presence attracted me strongly, and I quickly understood that it was mutual. These people, who in many ways are still unknown to me, chose me out of instinct. I can still hear their eager call for relationship: "Do you want to be our friend?" It was that call that led me to live in community with them.

The Small Inner Voice: My Ariadne's Thread

Over time, I discovered, through my interest in the writings of Vatican II, all that the Council fathers had written on the small inner voice that lives in the heart of each person: "Conscience is the most secret core and sanctuary of a man. There he is alone with God, Whose voice echoes in his depths" (*Gaudium et spes*, no. 16). What constitutes our dignity is the sacred shrine where God speaks to us to show us the way to good, and to turn us away from evil. This small voice does not issue orders. It proceeds above all from an intuition, an attraction to the God of love whom we can follow or reject in total freedom. It wants to lead us towards what is just and true, towards the love of the Gospel. Etty Hillesum said this in fitting words: "If I listen in all sincerity to my inner voice, I will know when the time comes if a man is sent to me by God ... and this inner voice must be my only Ariadne's thread." From a Christian perspective, this soft whisper echoes the gift of the Paraclete, the Holy Spirit. Gradually, I understood that this small voice within guided my most important decisions, from my joining the Navy to the creation of L'Arche.

I would even say that it is my way to freedom. Freedom is learning to listen to that inner voice, often in profound solitude.

It is learning to ignore other voices that oppose it: the desire for recognition, the willingness to conform to certain standards or appearances, the lure of power, the obsession with winning, laziness, fears… everything that strengthens my ego. To nurture this small voice, much listening, silence and work on oneself is required. Gandhi, in his complete works, highlights the need for "serious discipline" to be able to hear it and to recognize that it is authentic. That is true for all major decisions in life. But it is also true for everyday decisions: daring to speak freely, even when that goes against the flow and we risk being rejected or seen as an intruder.

I Had Found a Home

It was time.

My small voice had shown me the road to take. At first, it was just a whisper. But this whisper was persistent. And soon it was a certainty that swept away everything in its path. I had to live in Trosly.

With it came a slightly mad idea: What if I created a small, family-style community with a few people who had an intellectual disability? Fr. Thomas could accompany us – he was the one who helped me understand, through his own experience of suffering, that the hearts of the poor and the marginalized were more open to grace. Dr. Préaut encouraged me with great enthusiasm.

In the 1960s, these people were often shut up in asylums or psychiatric hospitals. The lucky ones stayed, at times with great difficulty, with their families. My dream of "living" with the poor in the name of Jesus – and not just "doing good" to them – seemed possible in this corner of Picardie where everything was leading me. My fate, I sensed, would be linked to these beings who are so often oppressed.

We must recall that many people, even today, see those with an intellectual disability as a horror to be eliminated and a source of shame for families. In the Gospel, the disciples, in the presence of a man blind from birth, ask Jesus a question: Was it because of his own sins or those of his parents that this man was born with a disability (John 9:2)? Jesus answers that there is no question of sin. If the man was born this way, it is so that God's works can be revealed. In our wealthy societies, we often seek to get rid of the most fragile members, and even kill them before they are born. For me, living with people with a disability offered new meaning: I gradually discovered that these situations, which are often seen as a horrible evil, open up a path towards God.

Wanting to better understand what disability is, I visited an institution in Saint-Jean-les-Deux-Jumeaux, in eastern France. How sad! Initially designed for around 40 patients, the place could barely hold double that number. Eighty men with intellectual disabilities were squeezed into this institution. I found people who were psychologically battered, even though the staff's generosity was not in question. My feelings swung between horror and fear. The residents were developing in an atmosphere of violence and terrible boredom. What I saw greatly distressed me. And yet, I felt mysteriously confirmed in my call to live with the most fragile, to be one with their immense human poverty. It was in Saint-Jean that I became friends with two residents, Raphaël Simi et Philippe Seux, who are at the origins of L'Arche. Raphaël, age 36, had contracted meningitis as an infant, causing him to lose his ability to talk and weakening his body. Philippe, age 22, had had viral encephalitis leading to paralysis in one arm and one leg. Unlike Raphaël, he could express himself easily. Both men had lost their parents. Because the institution was in the spotlight for failure to comply with care standards, I invited Raphaël and Philippe to come and live with me, with the director's approval.

That summer, I had bought, with the help of some friends, a dilapidated house in the village of Trosly, not far from Val fleuri and Fr. Thomas. There was no toilet or bathroom. We had to buy all the essentials: beds, furniture, appliances… Jacqueline, Fr. Thomas's secretary, helped me to buy these things and to make the little house – poor and simple as it was – a pleasant and welcoming place. Dr. Préaut took the necessary administrative steps so this small community scheme could be recognized as a foster care unit that was under Val fleuri. And that is how we settled in, Raphaël, Philippe and me, assisted for the first two weeks by a friend of Fr. Thomas's. Two others soon joined me: Henri, on August 22, and a bit later, Louis.

My life in Trosly was unusual in more ways than one. Where would it lead me? I had no idea. But for the first time, I had found a home. This place that God wanted me to find, towards which I had been moving for so many years, was right before my eyes. Since leaving the Navy in 1950, my life had been in a holding pattern. In Trosly, with Raphaël and Philippe, and all those who would arrive later, I felt I had found my place.

That is how L'Arche was quietly born. In poverty and simplicity. I gave up a university career in Canada, as I had given up my Navy officer's braids. And I was near Fr. Thomas. Far from the halls of academe, I allowed myself to be moulded by the simplicity of community life, with the oppressed and rejected. The joy I found there exceeded everything I could have imagined. And once again, great inner freedom was given to me.

A Sign of the Covenant

L'Arche… Jacqueline helped me find this name when it was time to baptize our fledgling community. In English, "Arche" means "Ark"; like Noah's Ark, L'Arche was dedicated to welcoming all sorts of fragile beings. An Ark that would be "the sign of the covenant that I make between me and you and every living creature that is with you, for all future generations" (Genesis 9:12). This Word of God embodies perfectly the joy we had in living together. Raphaël and Philippe seemed so happy to have left the institution and its atmosphere of violence. Often, in the morning, we would go into town to do our shopping. Back at the house, we would get to work in the kitchen. Then we would sit down at the table. The meal was the high point of our shared life. And, dare I say it, a moment of grace. Jesus said:

> "When you give a luncheon or a dinner, do not invite your friends or your brothers or your relatives or rich neighbours, in case they may invite you in return, and you would be repaid. But when you give a banquet, invite the poor, the crippled, the lame, and the blind. And you will be blessed, because they cannot repay you." (Luke 14:12-14)

In Trosly, we savoured the joy of the Gospel, as Pope Francis invites us to do today. The heart of our daily life gravitated around the table. Oh, the meals! Moments of pure joy. We roared with laughter. We gave free rein to our mischief, always ready for games and fun. Although people with an intellectual disability are unable to develop their rational intelligence, they have a heart that longs for encounter. Instead of having intense scholarly discussions, we spent our time sharing, joking and laughing. These moments were celebrations. Everyone was seeking happiness. No more and no less. Here, they knew they were accepted and loved with their weaknesses and their qualities, free to be themselves and to enjoy life. I let myself be carried along with it. In the morning, as soon as I could, I prayed alone with Jesus. After the evening meal, we got into the habit of praying the rosary together. The days passed happily.

Until then, I had led a rather austere existence, in the Navy or in my monastery visits, or in doing my doctorate in philosophy. I'm sure I gave the impression of being a serious and introverted man. If I dared, I would go so far as to say that it was at L'Arche that I learned to celebrate. Of course, when I am at table, I am a guide, the person in charge. But I am not above playing the clown. Here, my inner heart was revealed. The early days of the community were marked by this infectious and noisy joy, which attracted more and more people to our venture.

All these moments bring out my inner child. The one who likes to laugh and joke, rejoices in the little things, dares to be silly. Roadblocks of seriousness crumbled thanks to my new friends. A communion of hearts, in a new freedom, was revealed to us. We lived then what is still today the foundation of L'Arche: celebration and joy. I dare to say that we taste the joy and blessing of the kingdom of God promised by Jesus: "Blessed are you who are poor, for yours is the kingdom of God" (Luke 6:20 and Matthew 5:3).

13

Strength and Perseverance

March 1965. Dr. Préaut asked me to take on immediate responsibility for Val fleuri, the centre where Fr. Thomas was chaplain, 300 metres from our little community. Almost all the staff had quit due to tensions with the board of directors – a salary dispute. Although I felt at ease with the family scale of our little Ark, what awaited me at Val fleuri looked to be a far greater challenge. More than 30 men with an intellectual disability lived there. There I would be the head of an institution governed by strict standards – salaries, schedules, regulations... My administrative skills were patchy, to say the least. I felt lost, very poor in the face of this challenge. Also, the residents were unpredictable, prone to erupting into violence at any given moment. Broken windows were common. In many ways, it was a place of chaos. What should I do? Fr. Thomas encouraged me to accept this responsibility and sent me someone to support me on the administrative level. I accepted, with much trepidation.

Doubtless I needed to experience this other aspect of life with people affected by a disability: it was a kind of struggle that tested all my strength, my perseverance as well as my hope. A peaceful life of prayer here was out of the question. Authentic encounters, even more so. Luckily, I ate dinner every evening at L'Arche with Raphaël, Philippe and others. It was good for our community and necessary for me. At Val fleuri, I received support from a well-known psychiatrist, Dr. Léone Richet, from the Clermont psychiatric hospital in Oise. Dr. Richet provided constant support. Her medical knowledge was a great help. As much as my first encounter with disability at L'Arche left me with a feeling of joy and vitality, my experience at Val confronted me with difficulty, fear and violence. Through these clashes, I learned a lot about human suffering, about the anger of people touched by great weakness. So many of them were placed in a psychiatric setting by their families and experienced this situation as abandonment.

After about five years and thanks to the constant support of assistants who were convinced of the value and beauty of people with a disability, order and peace finally reigned at Val fleuri. French and Canadian volunteers arrived one after the other to lend us a hand. Thanks to them, the daily load was lightened. The period at Val was less a time of freedom and peace than an awareness of my own weaknesses, but also, ironically, of my inner freedom. When I arrived, I felt unable to cope. Yet I had to overcome these difficulties. Where did this strength come from? From Jesus, is all I can say. I am never alone because I know people are praying for me.

I understood then that L'Arche cannot only be a place of joy, just as it cannot only be a place of violence or difficulties. L'Arche is first of all a place where people with a disability yearn for a real encounter. For a heart-to-heart, I would even say. I, in turn, sensed a new desire to go towards the other. I had come here to live the Gospel, resolved to struggle peacefully against injustices because of Jesus. But I realized that Raphaël and Philippe, like their peers at Val fleuri, were filled with a powerful desire for encounter. They needed friends, not just professionals. Most of them had been oppressed, cast aside. Most of them had not even been allowed to live with their families. They longed for relationship: for relationships that helped them feel secure and helped them discover that they are lovable, that their humanity, although wounded, has value in our eyes.

14

Freedom to Grow

After we merged the two boards of directors, L'Arche ended up absorbing Val fleuri. Over time, we bought new houses in the village so we could welcome more people who had been shut away in psychiatric or other institutions. Jacqueline, an artist and painter, but above all a practical woman, looked after the arrangements and the décor for these houses. And so L'Arche grew. Deep within me, I sensed the growth of this desire, almost a passion, to respond to the cry of so many people who had been locked away, tormented by oppression and suffering. Friends came from France, and many from Canada, to strengthen our little community, which on a number of fronts seemed to be faltering, but radiated with joy. The idea of living in community with the poor, in the name of faith, seemed to attract many young people who were motivated by the impetus of the Second Vatican Council, which ended in 1965.

In many countries, during the 1960s and 1970s, people of all ages longed to live the community ideal, freed from the burden of heavy authority. Others sought, through these new ways of living, political expression, which erupted with the student protests in Paris in May 1968. A great need for liberation was making itself heard. Different attempts took shape here and there, even if not all of them were heading in the right direction. I suppose I was caught up in this pioneering movement.

It was a favourable time to start a new kind of community. But at L'Arche, people with a disability pointed us in the right direction.

A couple of Canadian Anglicans are a good example of the blossoming of these years: amazed by their stay at Trosly, they returned to Toronto to found an Anglican ecumenical L'Arche community in a house provided by some religious sisters after a retreat I gave in 1968. Soon after, a disciple of Mahatma Gandhi wrote to me to find out how to start a house in India. I agreed to go there, to assess the chances of such a plan. Miracle of miracles, barely a year later, an interfaith L'Arche named Asha Niketan was opened in Bangalore, in the south of India, thanks to the persistent intelligence of the person who took charge. Other communities began in Haiti, Ivory Coast, Burkina Faso, Honduras, England, Belgium and elsewhere, often following retreats dedicated to Jesus and the poor that I was invited to give around the world. What an incredible time! The unexpected led me here and there – the wonders never ceased. I felt myself being carried by the breath of the Spirit and by the prayer of many friends, especially the Carmelite Sisters. God, through L'Arche, wanted to make known the message of people with a disability in the churches and in the countries where we opened houses. They have a privileged place in the body of Christ, the Church, and in the whole human family. I spent a lot of time in airplanes and airports. Men and women joined us and got involved. Houses were opened. Money fell from the skies… Yes, it was an unsettling time. As if God had chosen me in spite of myself, with my weaknesses, to steer the ship. I felt more and more fulfilled, but also exhausted by this pace. In 1976, I was ordered to take two months of bed rest at Cochin hospital in Paris. Despite this setback, I was happy to see that the work was spreading throughout the world. The joy I find in people with a disability injects me with great strength, an irresistible momentum. I could also say much about the men and women who worked as assistants in the homes, or the members of our international board, who get involved with as much faith as wisdom and generosity. Strong friendships resulted. L'Arche's approach to governance, collaborative volunteers, forces me to be attuned to the views of others and to community events. It seemed to me that God used every detail to show us the road we should take. I learned little by little, at my expense, what it means to lead: serving life by getting out of the way. Together, we realized that L'Arche is truly a work of God and does not belong to us. It was beyond us. It was about discerning the reality, and following attentively and humbly the paths that opened before us. It is an experience of life, and not a prefabricated idea, that guides our steps.

My stay at the hospital in Paris made me realize that if I was working for the good of others, I also had to take care of myself. My unhealthy body was crying: Stop! Take care of me! Burnout is without a doubt the illness of the generous.

They do a lot for others, they give and they give, but they don't always know how to receive. People who are generous must learn to stop to welcome the joy of encounter and communion with the other, and agree to be transformed by the one they are caring for. Like I needed to do. The hospital helped me become more free. Doing too much had taken me away from my mission, from living more intimately with Jesus, and perhaps from greater attention to the small inner voice.

15

An Open Spirituality

"Following life" led L'Arche to new territory where we some-times felt alone. We weren't trying to be ecumenical or interfaith – it just happened through the movement of life. The first community, in Trosly, with Fr. Thomas there, was rooted in the Catholic Church. The second was born on Anglican soil, in Toronto. The third opened near Cognac, in a Catholic area. The fourth was in Bangalore and had contact with Hinduism, Sikhism and Islam. Our members reflected this diversity. Difficulties arose fairly quickly in the homes and sometimes also in international gatherings: How could we help each person to remain faithful to their own spirituality, their own religion, without offending those who believed something different? How could people of different faiths pray together?

At the beginning, L'Arche included many Catholics. We could tend to forget that not everyone shared our faith. Was L'Arche a Catholic project, open to other traditions, or a community that was intrinsically ecumenical and interfaith? That was the big question. In India, as in Canada, retreats were organized by the communities early on. How could we allow everyone to find their place, to be themselves, with no risk of proselytism? It was a long process. Other questions arose over time: Was Eucharistic sharing possible between Anglicans and Catholics at L'Arche? How could we make sure that people with a disability did not suffer from the inability to share Communion? Welcoming the needs of all is a long-term process. We learned, through our mistakes, of course, to live this ecumenical and interfaith dialogue harmoniously, encouraging each person to deepen their own religion, to live the essentials of their faith: seeking God by loving their brothers and sisters deeply. In this way, we were always vigilant when it came to the temptation of syncretism. Of course, there is a real risk of watering down the spirituality of others for the benefit of vague and consensual fraternal values. This issue will never be resolved. Above all, it stems from what is private. Being at L'Arche, living with the weakest and the poorest, means that each person must find a way to grow in love, beyond denominational affiliation, true to their own faith. That has not stopped some of our communities from feeling isolated. In Bangladesh, where the majority of people are Muslim, the imams still refuse to accept L'Arche with its identity. The Catholic Church has trouble considering it significant. Often, our communities feel like they are the only one of their kind. But we know that God loves everyone and calls each person to grow in love. God is hidden in the hearts of the little ones, the ones who experience the greatest suffering, the greatest oppression. Little by little, L'Arche became a sign of that love. Being open to all, faithful to each person's roots, is not always easy to live.

Ecumenism does not make a lot of noise. We are not the only ones to live this adventure. How can we forget Brother Roger Schutz of Taizé, who was so brutally taken from us in 2005? I have a special affection for the brothers of Taizé. This community in France is a ray of hope for our world. The links between L'Arche and Taizé have deep roots. In particular, the brothers of Taizé supported the launch of our community in Bangladesh.

Connections between L'Arche and the Anglican Church are also strong. In 1998, I was invited to speak to 800 bishops at the Lambeth Conference in England. More recently, Archbishop Justin Welby, head of the Anglican Communion, invited me to a meeting with the primates of the Anglican Church. During the closing Eucharist, we washed each other's feet in profound silence.

Beyond the Christian world, our communities enter into dialogue with believers around the globe. In India, our links to Hinduism were strengthened thanks to Pierre Ceyrac, S.J. (1914–2012), a remarkable man who devoted himself to the poor and the marginalized. His example continues to inspire us. Here is what Dr. Reddy, a Hindu, former chair of the Asha Niketan association (L'Arche in India), wrote to me on this subject: "Yes, in truth, God is our home. Dwelling in God and letting God awaken in us should be the goal of our entire life. This should be what we aspire to. And the only way to achieve this is to live in total abandonment to the divine. To give ourselves with all our being."

The current international coordinator of L'Arche is Stephan Posner. I admire him very much. This Jewish man has our mission pinned to his heart. Despite the walls that rise up, our community is called to undertake a path of unity and fraternity among all people. In Beirut, Nayla Tabbara and Fadi Daou dared to found an unprecedented interfaith centre in the sensitive context of the Middle East. Nayla is a Sunni Muslim theologian; Fadi is a Maronite priest. Both are committed to peace and reconciliation. They have given the world a book on divine hospitality that moved me deeply.[1] At our request, Nayla greatly helped the Muslims in our communities to discover the spirituality of L'Arche.

Not long ago, someone asked me, "You are Catholic; how can you live in communion with Jews and Muslims?" It's because of my love for Jesus: he is my friend and my model. He loves everyone, no matter their culture, their religion, their abilities or inabilities. Isn't there a danger, at times, that the Catholic Church hides Jesus, through its insistence on rules, at the expense of a real encounter with him?

---

1   *Divine Hospitality: A Christian–Muslim Conversation* (Geneva: WCC Publications, 2017).

16

A Free Electron

The growth of L'Arche had its struggles and misunderstandings. I started on my own. Of course, Fr. Thomas was there as a priest, but I was alone with Raphaël and Philippe. I asked the bishop of Beauvais for nothing. I told him of our presence and of our Christian vision, and he was happy about it. Then L'Arche started to spread into ecumenical and interfaith territory. For me, this came from the Holy Spirit. We moved forward together in great freedom, not asking anyone's permission, but informing the bishops of the places where we opened houses. What mattered was hearing the cry of the poor and responding to that cry as best we could. The religion of the person crying didn't matter. It was a deeply human cry, awakening the cry of my own heart, and that of many other men and women.

At the same time, I felt anchored in the Catholic faith, linked to the Church with every fibre of my being. At one point, with the growth of L'Arche on several continents, it seemed natural to meet with representatives of the Pontifical Council for the Laity in Rome. It was 1976, and our reception was fairly chilly:

"Is L'Arche Catholic?"

"Yes and no. Most of us are Catholic, but others are Protestant, Anglican, Hindu, Muslim…"

"Then there's no point in talking to us."

I felt during this meeting a certain rigidity of the Church towards us. L'Arche didn't fit into a box that had been established by canon law.

Later, a new president was appointed to the Pontifical Council for the Laity, Cardinal Eduardo Francisco Pironio. He welcomed me warmly. "Your work comes from the Holy Spirit. Whatever you do, keep going!" Later, he became a valuable adviser for L'Arche at the Vatican. He confirmed me and he confirmed L'Arche's unique path. Even today, I sometimes ask myself: Is there a danger that legal texts, although at times necessary, stifle the work of the Holy Spirit and the cry of the poor?

The fact that L'Arche did not fit into an existing category and that I felt welcomed by Cardinal Pironio helped me to accept this status of a free electron, unlike other leaders of communities who, after a while, ended up feeling stifled by overly restrictive rules. It was Cardinal Stanisław Ryłko, who succeeded Cardinal Pironio as head of the Pontifical Council for the Laity, who suggested that we propose the name of a bishop who was close to L'Arche as accompanying bishop for L'Arche Catholics with the Vatican. At our request, Bishop Pierre d'Ornellas accepted this mission. Gradually, we developed friendships with some bishops who agreed to support our ecumenical and interfaith approach. Beyond our institutional mission, some felt close to us by way of the heart. That was the case with Bishop Gérard Daucourt, emeritus bishop of Nanterre, who often visited us and whom we affectionately called in French our "Arche-évêque".

But I admit that beyond those few clergy who were close to our communities, especially the priests of L'Arche, few people in the Church understood our charism. Many applauded us, saying: "You are doing good work by welcoming the poor." For me it was not about doing good work, but revealing a path of life, a path to God. People with an intellectual disability are not poor little things we need to take care of. They are messengers from God who bring us closer to Jesus. They are a path to God. If we enter into relationship with them, they transform us and lead us to God. Cardinal Ryłko said: "L'Arche has caused a Copernican revolution." I must add that few theologians grasped this revolution. The first were the Anglican David Ford, who was dean of the faculty of theology at Cambridge, and Francis Young, a Methodist pastor and vice president of the University of Birmingham. David Ford once said something to us that I have never forgotten: "You have a good spirituality. But a good spirituality needs a good theology." And he helped us to deepen this reflection. Others, like Fr. Christian Salenson, emeritus director of the Institut de sciences et de théologie des religions in Marseille, and Fr. Étienne Grieu, a Jesuit at the Centre Sèvres in Paris, allowed us to go even further to deepen our theological and spiritual vision.

17

The Gospel in India

As I mentioned, L'Arche's fourth community opened in Bangalore in 1970. It all began with a letter from an Indian man who was involved in the social world. He had heard about our work and wanted us to come to India. So Mira and Gabrielle, two members of our community, left in October 1969 to prepare for my visit and my upcoming Indian lectures. I joined them in December. We had been given an excellent property not far from the Bangalore psychiatric hospital. In September 1970, after a series of steps, L'Arche opened its doors.

Two years later, Gabrielle suggested that we go to Calcutta, India's largest city, where we met with Cardinal Lawrence Picachy. He had heard with interest about L'Arche's mission – to the point of offering us a small diocesan house, which looked perfect for a L'Arche home. That is when I met Mother Teresa, who was world renowned for having founded the Missionaries of Charity two decades earlier. Their charism was relieving the suffering of the poorest of the poor, especially those dying in the streets. We became friends right away. Mother Teresa helped me understand the Indian reality from within, like the day she took me to a neighbourhood in Calcutta crowded with a million refugees. They had all fled the armed conflict between Pakistan and Bangladesh. I visited several of these hospices, and it was very moving. Mother Teresa did exceptional work.

When I lived in Calcutta, I went to mass every day at the sisters' novitiate. Mother Teresa was always there, wrapped in silence. Her face, weathered by fatigue, shone with her love of prayer and of God. After mass, she often invited me to breakfast. The sisters made delicious eggs, and God knows it was hard to find them in Calcutta. Together, we talked about this and that. Mother Teresa shared with me her desire to add a new branch to her community for Hindu women: she had gotten the green light from Rome. These women would remain true to their own faith while putting on the Missionaries of Charities' habit to work with the poorest people. Mother Teresa asked me to give a retreat for them. Sadly, this interfaith project never came to fruition.

In the mid-1980s, Cardinal Picachy, who had welcomed us so enthusiastically, left the Archdiocese of Calcutta to retire. His successor demanded that L'Arche give up the diocesan house, which in the meantime had been promised to Mother Teresa's sisters. Finding a house that met our needs in this desperately poor city was not easy. Weeks passed; we were unable to pack up and move. Mother Teresa seemed especially angry.

"The Archbishop is very unhappy because you are still in the house, and you are preventing our sisters from moving in."

"But Mother," I replied, "it's impossible! We can't find another house for our severely disabled members."

"Listen," she said, exasperated, "I'll give you a property."

That is how Mother Teresa gave us a lovely property in a quiet part of Calcutta. The lot abutted another one, which she had set aside for former prostitutes who were re-entering society after serving their sentences. A third property, adjoining the other two, was intended as a home for criminals and addicts. I have to say that this combination surprised me very much.

> "You know what will happen… The criminals will sooner or later climb over the wall to go and see the former prostitutes!"

> "You will stop them."

> "No, Mother, that's your job, not mine."

This infamous property would finally go to religious who were in formation… Ah, Mother Teresa! The entire nature of this holy woman had a profound effect on me. Our friendship meant a lot to me. It was and remains a light, given completely to people of the street and the poorest of all, no matter what their culture or religion. Her example remains relevant for younger generations. She is now Saint Mother Teresa.

India was the place where I saw the most extreme poverty. Slums as far as the eye could see. Sickness and death everywhere. And in the midst of it all, a people who overflowed with kindness. From one encounter to the next, the richness of Hindu spirituality enlightened me. Thanks to the people of India, I could appreciate Gandhi's thought. What a wise man! He was able to free India from the British yoke without ever disparaging the value of human beings. Gandhi was a universal brother. He worked for the untouchables, whom he called *harijan*, which means children of God. Renouncing all violence, Mahatma Gandhi told us to love our enemies to give them the opportunity for inner transformation, in exploring the meaning of universal values. This extraordinary man introduced non-violence to the modern world: an essential path towards reconciliation and universal peace. Thanks to Mahatma, this is at the heart of L'Arche teaching. In the United States, Martin Luther King was one of the most impressive disciples.

Still in India, another witness to the Gospel became a great friend of L'Arche: the Jesuit Pierre Ceyrac. This priest who was for and close to the poor helped us very much as we became established locally, especially in Chennai, formerly Madras, in the south of India. He also nurtured our spiritual vision, in contact with Hinduism and Indian realities.

I would like to conclude this story by paying tribute to Fr. Andrew Travers-Ball, who by Mother Teresa's side founded the men's branch of the Missionaries of Charity in 1963. He was an exceedingly good and gentle man.

We are indebted to him for his wonderful work, even though personal battles kept him from his mission as founder for a long time. As his community grew, Brother Andrew was overcome by exhaustion and stress. He sought escape from his troubles in alcohol and gambling. He suffered terribly. The new head of the Order kicked him out. I was devastated, as I loved Brother Andrew. I remember the day when he took me by motorcycle through the bumpy streets of Calcutta to show me the darkest and most infamous corners, where his commitment began. We lost touch when he fell into the abyss, and I regretted that. But little by little, he got back on his feet. His spiritual life blossomed once again. And then, by chance, we reconnected. I saw before me a man of exceptional holiness, who exuded goodness. What a lesson in the spiritual life! Here was a man who had fallen into the pit. But he got up again, in total humility. The letters we exchanged bear the imprint of a beautiful soul. I feel lucky to have crossed paths with Brother Andrew.

18

Community: A Place of Healing and Liberation

L'Arche started with three people. We simply lived together. Then the community grew. I learned a lot from those who joined us day after day. After eight years of solitude, from 1956 to 1964, this life with others broadened my horizons. I discovered that I needed them. Community life was liberating. It liberated me from being turned in on myself, and opened me to the beauty of others. L'Arche is a new form of community. If you want to reduce the walls that separate people, groups and races, walls that create fear and hatred, you have to be together. A community saves us from a fierce individualism and a sense of isolation; it gives us security and brothers and sisters who agree to live the encounter. It encourages personal freedom and growth towards true human fullness. It prevents us from being trapped in a sectarian group. A community is a place where women and men live an authentic relationship and work together on a common mission.

The mission, for L'Arche, is the well-being and growth of people who are weaker, who are marginalized because of intellectual difficulties or disabilities. This mission cannot be fulfilled unless a life of relationship brings people with disabilities together with assistants. The heart of L'Arche is in the encounter of persons who commit to intertwining their lives – some have more abilities and are stronger, but have human weaknesses and problems; others are weaker and have fewer abilities on an intellectual level, but have a real capacity for growth.

Our world creates a strong feeling of isolation for many people. No doubt these are the limits of a prevailing culture that pushes us towards individual success. Success is seen as the only valid guarantee of improvement and recognition. Sometimes, this logic leads some fragile people, who need security, to join groups that are closed, sectarian even, in which they lose their freedom.

L'Arche is the opposite. A true community, as I define it, is a place of belonging that helps each person, each member, to become themselves and become more free. It is a place where hearts and minds are healed, where what is deepest in each person can awaken and grow according to their individual gifts. Belonging for becoming. Our communities try to nurture a fruitful relationship among all members, united in the same mission. That is something beautiful and elusive, and must be done continually.

*

As you can imagine, daily life at L'Arche also includes some practical things. Living together involves rules, schedules and, of course, finances – finding ways to survive financially and meeting with those who fund us. People with disabilities change and get older. So do the assistants. Not to mention the work of organizing our workshops in the homes. Doctors and psychiatrists support us. All this for the good of each person and to help each person find their place. But for me, the essential part is the joy of being together, because many people who come to

L'Arche will live there for the rest of their lives. Assistants get involved with L'Arche by responding to a vocation. Some are married, and some are single "for the kingdom," while others are still seeking. Some are paid and commit for a long time, inspired by a vision of the covenant, a covenant that connects people with each other, in God. Others will seek adventure in other communities. Still others volunteer for shorter periods. For all, the heart of the community is in the relationship with the weakest and in celebration, the joy of being together. Our presence shows that men and women of various cultures, religions and abilities can live in community an experience of unity around one mission. In spite of differences. In spite of each person's abilities and lack of abilities. In a world where so many walls are still being put up, where divisions, war and hatred harden hearts, we want to be the sign of fellowship that is possible between the men and women of this earth. Peace is not out of reach. Of course each of us, individually, must change.

It is the spirituality of L'Arche to help each person to grow in a greater and more authentic love, to knock down the walls in our hearts so we can accept – not because we have to, but in recognition of – different people with their temperaments and cultures. Looking beyond the other's inabilities and temperament. Looking at the heart. That is freedom. All people have, deep down, a great desire to love, even if the ego sometimes weighs down this desire. Of course there are difficulties. Of course there are tensions. That is human. Love involves forgiveness. Growing in a human way means learning to forgive over and over, and it is a daily struggle. But it is a gentle struggle, with oneself and in one's relationships.

✳

Love – seeing the other as deeply respectable and valuable – can grow only with time and through difficulties. Isn't it essential to work on ourselves to overcome the barriers, the fears, the blockages we carry? To break free of our irritation when it comes to the other's culture, faults and character to work for the shared mission? To free us from our desires that are centred on ourselves? This love is called to grow all the time. The spirituality of L'Arche gives us the energy we need to love more every day. And love, for a Christian, means loving as Jesus loves. Even loving our enemies… We have to discover this path of faith. For many, this spirituality is nurtured by prayer and the Eucharist. For others, it may be in times of meditation and silence, as part of religious faith or something else. It also involves developing wisdom. Each person learns to dig this trench within them and discover the inner voice there, which will help them grow in love. That is the mystery of L'Arche. And perhaps this is the most important thing, in the end, for every human person. Growing to love wisely those who are different, with ever more kindness, listening and truth. In his book *Understanding Pope Francis*, Andrea Riccardi, founder of the Sant'Egidio community, claims that a community is rooted in a known history and is oriented towards the hope of a utopia. And the utopia is found beyond the immediate mission. It is found in love and universal peace, joy and God's plan. Pope Francis says utopia is the unwavering belief that another world is possible.

The signs of true community are seen in the joy and the quality of celebrations that reveal mutual love. This joy springs up from the freedom of the members, who are aware of the meaning and importance of their shared mission. It is a utopia that inspires. And it is a hope that emerges. The community involves a certain quality of conversation among members, casual encounters allowing each one to speak and be heard. Being able to share in small groups, humbly and truthfully, what we are living, where we are at. Being able to express what unites us internally and what increases our love for our shared mission.

A community that takes care of its weaker members will always be weak, because it always involves the arrival of new members. Often they lack training and experience; they need a lot of support and help to understand the community's vision and mission. How do we unify the institution and the community? Our communities are accredited institutions and are sometimes funded by the state. How can we combine professionalism and love? To be truly competent, we must love the other. Competence without love can become destructive. Love without competence can become emotional. How can we be ecumenical and interfaith and help each person deepen their own faith? How can we combine faith in Providence and good human planning? How can we reconcile justice and mercy? The answer to all these questions lies in a deepening of the vision and in the heart of each member of the community: growing in a love that unites each person from within, and helping it to be a source of unity and peace in the community and in society.

19

Authority through Listening

A community needs to be governed and guided by a leader: the servant of the community and of the mission. I needed time to learn how to exercise authority at L'Arche. In the Navy, I learned to obey without discussion and also to command. When we started in Trosly, there were only a handful of us. Raphaël and Philippe tasted the joy of having left the bleak institution where they had lived for so many years. I myself experienced great joy with them. Of course, I was still very conscious of helping them to flourish and grow. Authority involved assuming this responsibility as best I could: allowing each person to be themselves in their weakness and their gifts – not trying to forcing them into a mould. In the home, there were no rules as such. There was life. Authority had to foster that. But L'Arche grew. And I had to ensure that this life could continue. People from all over joined us as assistants. A community organization became necessary. The essence of authority happened through a personal relationship. Helping each person to be themselves, to be fulfilled and take on responsibilities, and I would even say to be free, by learning to recognize and listen to the small inner voice as a call from God.

Christmas 1965. The calm of an abbey near Trosly. Twenty assistants from Val fleuri and from L'Arche are with me. I suggest that we form three groups and discuss this question:

What, in our life at L'Arche, do we think is positive, and what leaves something to be desired?

For an hour, each person was able to speak freely. Then we came back together as a large group. I was amazed – and a bit shocked, I have to admit – at everything that was said about the weaknesses. I realized that I stayed too far removed from certain daily realities, and that things were not going as smoothly as they could between us. That is how our community council came to be. Its aim was to ensure good internal communication, better define each person's responsibilities, know who is responsible for whom and for what... After our discussion, we also drafted a constitution stating the practical arrangements of our life together, which had been rather vague until now. The mission of L'Arche is to help not only the weakest and the most marginalized to rise up – that is the key – but also each assistant. Exercising authority therefore lies in active listening. This is something that happens from the bottom up, not the other way around. Everything, in the mandate and in the organization, must lead to the healing, growth and blossoming of all the members, especially the weakest. Recently, our friends at Secours Catholique began a transformation that I find relevant. From now on, it's no longer about doing things for people in difficulty, but being with them. "Being with" is healing for everyone: for those who help and for those who receive it. Everyone is transformed. So authority is reversed, the opposite of all our usual models, just as Jesus knelt before his disciples. Two wonderful communities, founded recently by young adults, share this same idea of authority, which allows street people to live with volunteers: APA (Association pour l'Amitié) and Association Lazare are to me prophetic signs, like L'Arche and other associations. In Canada and elsewhere, the same kind of shared life is developing for elderly people, some of whom have dementia, who reconnect through a kind of family life. Others are oriented towards addicts, people with mental health issues. I am more and more convinced that these small communities where people live together, by agreeing to let themselves be transformed, will play a key role in the evolution of our societies. Isn't this a path of healing and conversion for each one of us?

20

When Faith Sets Our Hearts Free

At the beginning of 1969, Marie-Hélène Mathieu, a friend who established the Office chrétien des personnes handicapées (Christian Office for People with Disabilities) in Paris, came to see me in Trosly. Committed to serving people with a disability – especially an intellectual disability – Marie-Hélène attentively supported their families, who faced various difficulties. On that day, Marie-Hélène told me the story of a couple that had deeply touched her. Camille and Gérard Proffit had described to her their disastrous visit to Lourdes with their two children, Thaddée and Loïc, both of whom had intellectual disabilities. The four pilgrims were treated with hostility by the hotel staff. Their presence was seen as undesirable, as they were bluntly informed. The couple ended up leaving, badly scarred by the experience.

At that time, many people thought that those with an intellectual disability did not belong on pilgrimages. They were not able, it was believed, to experience a journey of faith. Their exuberance might bother other pilgrims. These were the prejudices that Camille and Gérard and their two children encountered. I listened to Marie-Hélène's story, moved by the distress the couple had expressed. What to do? We could not remain deaf to their cries. As the conversation unfolded, we had an idea: What if we were to organize a large pilgrimage for people with an intellectual disability, along with their families and friends?

＊

A small group was soon formed. "Faith and Light" was born. In the Church, our determination elicited some enthusiastic responses – but also some suspicion. Three years of painstaking preparation was needed. The gathering took place in 1971, on Easter weekend. At the foot of the grotto of Massabielle, more than 12,000 pilgrims flocked from all over France and beyond, with around 15 nationalities represented. There were 4,000 parents, the same number of people with a disability, and as many friends. How to describe the atmosphere of this rich multitude… I was speechless. Even today, I am amazed by all that we saw and heard. It was so special.

＊

In Lourdes, we made sure everyone felt welcome. We did not hesitate to adapt the liturgy for this unconventional audience. On Easter Sunday, after the Vigil and the Mass of Resurrection, we danced in the square of the shrine with indescribable joy. The celebration continued into the afternoon. We sang, did some impromptu mimes and played all sorts of games.

I remember the atmosphere of fellowship that prevailed in all these communities. Each group from the same region stayed in a hotel reserved for them. Hallways that were usually subdued bubbled with irresistible playfulness. In the streets, we rubbed shoulders with people with a disability as well as their parents and families, not to mention their friends, many of whom were also young and propelled by exuberant energy.

These were days of joy and unity. No one felt left out. Amazingly, the Marian aspect of the site did not dampen the ecumenical zest of our endeavour: Protestant pilgrims and their chaplains mingled with us.

On Easter Monday, before saying goodbye, we decided to gather one last time with all the regional leaders. "We can't stop here; we want to continue the adventure," they all said, gripped, like us, by the power of this foundational experience. Unable to predict the future, Marie-Hélène and I replied simply, "Keep gathering in your community, and we will see where the Holy Spirit wants to lead us." And that is how Faith and Light came to be…

✻

In 1975, Paul VI welcomed a large international pilgrimage of Faith and Light under the dome of Saint Peter's Basilica.

"You have a chosen place in the Church," he told us, confirming the particular vocation of the most fragile, the most neglected members of the human family.

Faith and Light now numbers around 1,500 communities in 85 countries. The movement is well developed in the Middle East, with 70 groups in Egypt alone. We had wonderful times in Syria, especially in Aleppo, before the civil war led to an exodus of tens of thousands of families… In France, 300 communities gather actively in a number of cities. Through all these years, our original idea has not changed. Our members, although they don't live under the same roof, get together two or three times a month. They take part in retreats, shared holidays and many other activities, spending time, like that first time, with people with an intellectual disability, their parents and their friends.

The spirit of our communities is based on this sharing of life, this unconditional welcome, in joy and simplicity.

That is how Faith and Light made L'Arche known and L'Arche made Faith and Light known. Our two forms of community are fed by the same spiritual vision. We learned over time that people with a disability are near to God. They have open hearts and a great desire for relationship. Many of them thrive upon discovering Jesus as a close friend. And in doing so, they show us a path. By their side, we understand that God chose the foolish and the weak to confound the strong and the intelligent. We understand that God chose the most despised to confound those who are trapped in their own heads.

21

Communion beyond Words

A t the end of the 1960s, I visited a few facilities in Sweden for people with an intellectual disability. One of them welcomed those with severe disabilities. Some of the residents could not speak or walk. And yet I was struck by the relational life that existed between these people with profound weaknesses and the assistants who cared for them. I was shocked to discover the possibility of a relationship with people who had such severe disabilities. It was clear to me: I had glimpsed another aspect of the vocation of L'Arche. Back in Trosly, I spoke about it to those around me. Gradually, we launched a plan to create three specialized homes: one in Trosly and two in Cuise-la-Motte. I entrusted the implementation of this project to Odile Ceyrac, assistant director of the community. She had done a placement with adolescents who had severe disabilities in the Clermont psychiatric hospital. From this experience she knew a number of young people who could benefit from a L'Arche home. All this took time. In the end, we got the approvals we needed. And so La Forestière was opened in April 1978. I remember this special day, and the feeling of celebration that floated through the streets of Trosly.

We welcomed Loïc, age 20 – the same young man who, a few years earlier, had inspired the founding of Faith and Light. You would have thought he was eight or 10. He could barely walk and could not speak at all. There was also Éric, who was blind and deaf, and unable to move his limbs. Psychologically, he was very fragile and deeply distressed. Joining them were Édith, Lucien and Marie-Jo. Despite her marked disability, Marie-Jo managed to get around in a wheelchair. Her only way of expressing herself was through a lot of screaming. Her violence took us aback: she would often slap herself in the face…

As the years passed, we realized that La Forestière was an essential place. The assistants who lived with people with severe disabilities found great joy there. When, in 1980, I stepped down from leadership of the community, I became an assistant at La Forestière. I slept there once a week, to care for one person or another who was suffering intense distress or finding it hard to sleep. I learned to live with each of them. And I have to admit that Éric, in particular, was a teacher for me. With the other members of the team, we bathed him every day. These were important moments – touching his body respectfully and gently. Éric had had a chaotic life; he was placed in a psychiatric hospital at age four. His mother, who had suffered greatly because of him, came to visit him once and then never returned. This woman had a lot of trouble accepting her child's suffering. Éric endured terrible anxiety – a feeling far greater than fear. We can be afraid of a dog or of a dark alley. But if the dog leaves or the alley brightens, we are no longer afraid. Anxiety stems from existential suffering. Who am I? Am I loved? I feel lost. No one wants me. I feel alone, abandoned. This anxiety arises from great inner tensions. Éric made a lasting impression on me by plunging me into this unknown universe. With him, language was no help, nor was visual interaction. It involved trying to understand him, especially through touch, by being attuned to his body language. Éric, Loïc and all the others taught me a lot about this. I discovered another degree of relationship, especially through the body. What Éric needed to feel was that he belonged to a group, a community, a family. We had to help him break down his solitude and his anxiety by helping him realize that he was important to us. Little by little, Éric understood that he was someone. He calmed down. We were able to consider surgery on his legs. And he started walking!

At night, after dinner, we put everyone in their pyjamas, then we spent some time together in prayer. Éric would sit on my lap or on the lap of another assistant. There, he could rest. Sometimes he even fell asleep there. With him, as with others, I experienced times of silent communion: the profound feeling that we were there for each other and that through this communion radiated great joy.

Those who do not speak, like Loïc, Marie-Jo and Éric, lead us to a deeper connection through the language they speak through their bodies. This means we must be attuned to each gesture they make, for the body becomes speech.

A friend of mine recently attended the baptism of a child in Paris. During the celebration, the priest showed that he was attuned to a few people with disabilities, members of the family of the baptized child. My friend went to see him to tell him how much his attitude towards the weakest had touched her. He replied, "You know, I was at L'Arche 20 years ago, and it was Loïc who taught and transformed me." At L'Arche, we must never forget this mysterious mission of the littlest ones. Those who knew Loïc are forever changed.

It was at La Forestière that I delved into the mystery of communion between people through their physical dimension. This silent communion is a source of peace. It does not possess the other, but gives them freedom. It finds its source in God – otherwise it can turn into fusion, possession of the other. Friendship can involve communion, but it is above all unity through speaking and sharing: we walk together towards a common goal. Fellowship involves deep respect for the other, for we belong to the same human family. These three realities – communion, friendship and fellowship – are the core meaning of L'Arche.

At La Forestière, I also became aware of my own weaknesses when it comes to relationship, and my difficulty in opening myself up to others in certain circumstances. And of my own violence. Lucien, one of the first members of this specialized home, had a serious psychic disability. He was separated from his mother and placed in a hospital when he was 30, when she became ill. This sudden isolation sent him into terrible anxiety. Finally, he was admitted to La Forestière. He was suffering greatly – screaming and screaming some more, sometimes for two hours straight. His high-pitched screams were almost unbearable for me. Before long, they awakened my own anguish. I felt powerless, bereft before Lucien. My anguish turned to anger, not only towards him but also towards myself, because the situation kindled in me some truths that were difficult to accept. It took very little, I realized, to see this anger turn into hate, into violence. Thank God I lived in community, and other assistants knew better than I how to offer Lucien help. It was not easy for me to comprehend this harsh and anxious world. No easier than it was to recognize how persistent the seeds of violence were in me and, we must admit, in every human being. Living at La Forestière in 1980–1981 was an important time for me: it helped me get to know myself better and accept myself as I am, to walk towards greater freedom.

22

Joy Is Tested

It was after I became responsible for Val fleuri that tensions arose between Fr. Thomas and me, beginning in 1965. As a religious, he had his own ideas of what L'Arche should be: a Catholic community centred on the poor. He had trouble with our administrative structures and the fact that we were an institution funded by the state. Of course, I had been shaped by his theological and spiritual vision of the poor: it is through the poor that we must approach Jesus and build the Church. However, we were having disagreements about practical matters during meetings of the community council, to which he belonged. The conflict increased when L'Arche became open to having an ecumenical and interfaith dimension, and then when the community spread to a village near Trosly. Even disbelief when we welcomed our first women with intellectual disabilities. Fr. Thomas was not comfortable with our development internationally, either. These tensions were hard for both of us to accept. There was a kind of clash between spiritual father and son, which I found painful. I didn't know how to work with or resolve this conflict, to find a deeper truth. I wanted to follow what the community council decided, even if that meant freeing myself from the thought of Fr. Thomas. Of course, I tried not to let these differences erupt, as I was concerned about preserving L'Arche and working towards unity.

Despite my suffering, my aggression, my lack of sensitivity towards Fr. Thomas, this tension helped me to grow. It forced me to find within myself a new confidence, a new freedom. But this conflict situation, combined with the great growth of L'Arche, presented me with an obvious temptation: giving into pride. If I sometimes hit this obstacle, it was never voluntarily. It doesn't take much for our certainties, so human, too human, to stifle the authenticity of our impulses while being ruled by our ego. L'Arche "succeeded," and the temptation was real. I was the first to be disturbed by this, just as I had been disturbed by my ongoing tensions with Fr. Thomas. I felt that I owed him so much. And yet, I admired him. Maybe I was naive. But the fact that L'Arche was born in Trosly was partly thanks to him. People came from far away to meet with him. Especially those who were suffering. The ambivalence of our relationship left me feeling guilty: I no longer felt in harmony with him, to the point that I stopped talking to him about my spiritual life, as I had done before; it was as if I was in conflict with a vocation he had helped me to give birth to, at least based on my own understanding. This caused me times of anguish that were hard to bear. As I have often said, my relationship with Fr. Thomas was a great joy and also a great trial, perhaps a greater trial than I took the time to realize. I was driven by a need for action and the desire to preserve unity in L'Arche.

*

In the twilight of my life, I learned that some women wanted to testify against Fr. Thomas about their suffering caused by his behaviour after the founding of L'Arche. Upon the request of the leaders of L'Arche, the Church – and this was a good thing – wanted to allow all people who had suffered in this way to be able to speak and be heard within the context of a canonical investigation. Their corroborating testimony revealed his sexual abuse of adult women, without disabilities, in a spiritual direction context. These behaviours caused serious harm to these women and were painful for L'Arche. When the testimony of these abused women was brought to my attention, I was shocked. Gradually, I had to accept this painful reality, which I knew nothing about until well after the death of Fr. Thomas. I felt anger. Then sadness… And almost disbelief: How was this possible? Had Fr. Thomas lost his mind? Deep down, there was a total rejection, a clear condemnation of the acts of abuse that these women reported. But even more, deep within me arose much compassion for the victims of these abuses. And yet, it was in part thanks to Fr. Thomas that L'Arche was born in Trosly. I still feel a painful disbelief in the face of this difficulty holding together these two truths. But I mourned Fr. Thomas. Going through this unexpected trial helped me to grow in freedom. In this mystery of suffering that L'Arche bears today, I turn my attention to those who were hurt, and I pray for them, that each one of them can gradually regain trust and peace in their hearts. I also pray that our communities and everyone in L'Arche today can patiently heal the wounds of their brothers and sisters. And I pray for Fr. Thomas. I pray that together, at the foot of the cross of Jesus, we can all be open to the mercy of God. That is the only reality that brings me peace and trust. L'Arche leads us all to welcome with love people with deep wounds.

23

Living with Our Weaknesses

For centuries, a disability was seen as divine punishment. A sense of shame, even rejection, gripped many parents, despite the wonderful and accepting hospitality of many others. With L'Arche and Faith and Light, we gradually learned that people with a disability have a special mission in the Church and in our societies. At the beginning, I thought I would carry out a Gospel work by trying to do them good. Isn't God closest to the poorest of all? Doesn't Saint Paul say that God chose the foolish and the weak, and even the most despised, to confound the wise and the strong? Over the years, I evolved as I discovered that it was these people who did me good and, more than that, changed me.

Why? The reason is simple. Their deepest cry is always born of an authentic desire to enter into relationship, and is never an individual quest for success, for upward social mobility. Nor do they aspire to conquer anything. This leads them to experience relationships in a unique way. Many of them have the heart of a child in an adult's body. And this heart longs to meet us in that place in us where the child lives, where a spring flows deep within us. People with a disability open a space in the consciousness of those who welcome their cry for relationship. Their presence gradually lowers the protective barriers that we have patiently erected to hide our vulnerabilities and our weaknesses, and to strengthen our sense of power. It leads to a true encounter, a distinctive and freeing heart-to-heart: a joyful communion. Their freedom to be "a little foolish," outside social standards for conforming, encourages us to also become a little foolish, freely. In leaving behind our saviour complexes, in ceasing to be the ones who know, we learn that these people who are weaker lift us up, humanize us and open us to God. They heal our instinct for cultural superiority. They help us to enter into what is essential in life.

It's not about always having more things, or achieving great things. It's about loving and recognizing the other who is different, and weaker, as someone important who has a mission on earth. The most fragile refresh the commandment of Jesus to love one another as he loves us. That is the heart of the mystery: we were created to welcome the weak for who they are, that is, people who are different, with their strengths and their weaknesses. Each one carries within them a source of life, a hidden primal innocence. Welcoming the weak implies that I gradually accept not only my strengths but also my own physical weaknesses, my faults, my mistakes, my lapses of attention… They are a path to a true encounter with myself and with the other.

I experienced a real transformation in living with people touched by great weakness. We tend to quickly place them, because of their vulnerability, at the bottom of the social scale. Too often, we even try to eliminate them before they are born. Yet they have much to teach us. It was in being in contact with their weakness that I began to welcome my own. In this way I was able to reach the depths of my heart, without needing to hide behind a mask of strength or goodness. We are all born in extreme weakness. We will all die in extreme weakness. All our lives, we have a fragile body that, at any moment, can be overtaken by illness or accident. And in the history of each person, there are these moral and spiritual weaknesses that lead us away from the truth and from real love. People with an intellectual disability may not grow intellectually, but they know better than anyone how to restore delight in our humanity. Learning to live with weakness, as well as with strength, turns our certainties and our desires for power upside down. And that is, I dare to say, a powerful leaven to lift up our societies. Is it utopian to want a world with greater fellowship, where I see the weak person as a brother or sister in humanity? Of course, the road is long. Outside of times of sharing with the people we welcome, I realized sadly that I carried more fears within me, and that my ego continued to lead me astray, as if at times I needed to prove my superiority, my importance, to exist.

Patience. And humility. That's all we need to eliminate our bursts of pride.

24

Freedom Hidden in
Those Who Are Oppressed

Pauline was 40 years old. She was a woman with a disability whom we welcomed at L'Arche in 1973. Due to having had encephalitis as a child, she had a paralyzed arm and leg. She had epilepsy, and she would have bouts of violence that challenged us as much as they frightened us. In time, I realized that her attitude stemmed from oppression she had suffered her whole life. People called her a retard, an idiot, etc. At home with her family. Then at school. And on the street, for 40 years… She came to hate her own battered body. Our psychiatrist, Erol Franko, pointed out to us that her violence was a cry: "Doesn't anyone want to be my friend?" It was a long road for a woman like Pauline to free herself from the spiral of oppression and a sense of guilt for existing, to rediscover confidence in herself. So many people with an intellectual disability have experienced similar bullying. This can sustain a kind of chronic violence, even deep depression. At La Ferme, our spiritual centre in Trosly, we organize retreats, sometimes for people who experience extreme oppression: homeless people, women trapped in prostitution, people who are gay, people who are divorced, separated and sometimes remarried. I confess that I feel especially touched by this world of the oppressed. I remember the young man who had just become aware of his attraction to men and the fear that women instilled in him. He cried. He cried because people at school made fun of him. He cried because he could feel his parents' lack of understanding and their hostility. Barely 50 years ago, homosexuality was an offence punishable with a prison sentence in Canada, and it remains so in a number of countries in Africa and the Middle East. Thanks to these deeply moving gatherings, a huge number of oppressed and fragile people were revealed to me, as if they were emerging from the shadows. These oppressions can arise out of rejection by the family, the Church or society, from a sense of guilt related to one's way of looking at a particular situation. Each of them, through their experience, lives something intense on a human level. We can learn a lot from these people, if we take the time to listen to them and encounter them. Each one carries their secret, their poverty and sometimes anger towards themselves. Because of their struggle, they reveal human truths that often elude us. In each of them resides a hidden beauty, primal innocence, a yearning for life that can take many years to blossom. In Pauline's case, it was a long road before she could build a positive self-image. That happened slowly; through various relationships with assistants, we were able to help her understand that "You are important to us." She had the right to exist as she was – free to be herself.

✳

It is always the need to dominate others or to satisfy our ego's cravings that prevents us from freeing those who are oppressed. This ego, revealed in the severity of our judgments, stops our true identity from awakening so we can encounter these people. It is sometimes difficult to fight it. Becoming free… We all want this. Once again, we must topple the barriers around our hearts. Remove the slag and the rubble that blocks the well at the depth of our being. Everything that imprisons us in the certainties of superiority, personally and in the groups we belong to, is called to disappear so we can enjoy our freedom as children of God, buried in our human poverty.

We who dread situations of oppression can learn so much from people who have been oppressed. We must go down to meet them. They offer us a privileged path to reach this truth. This encounter happens through shared presence, blessed communion. We must not be afraid to express the tenderness that is within us – to look at the other with goodwill and humility, without judging and condemning, and listening to their story. Saint Paul tells us what true love is (1 Corinthians 13). Patience. Service. Joy in truth. A love that bears all things, accepts all things, believes all things and hopes for all things. Who else but the Spirit of truth can inspire in us such love? A love capable of arousing the best and deepest in the wounded in life… Helping them to rediscover (or discover for the first time) confidence in themselves, and showing them that they are more beautiful than they dare to believe by receiving the gift of their life. We can only help another person to free themselves from their obstacles if we ourselves have undertaken a path to freedom in humility.

Discovering my own fortifications, my fears, created in me the desire to move forward. Hope, too. Six centuries before Jesus Christ, Buddha said, "A man who conquers himself is greater than one who conquers a thousand men in battle." Thanks to L'Arche, I understand that my own abilities are not enough to control my ego, which is entrenched below layers of secret fears. I need strength and a new presence of the Holy Spirit. I know that I must distinguish between how I use the gifts I have received and developed so I can carry out my mission, and my ego that pushes me to want to be better than others. "We must wage the hardest war, which is the war against oneself," points out Patriarch Athenagoras of Constantinople. "We must disarm ourselves. I am disarmed of the need to be right, and to justify myself by disqualifying others."

The encounter with those who are oppressed, the weakest, those who have lost all points of reference because of dementia, is life-changing. Conditioned by our desires to ascend, we understand that we must descend to encounter God hidden in them and in us. Meeting them allows us to discover God's invisible power and the sweetness of his presence.

In my case, it is not so much an inflated ego that prevents me from fully receiving strength from God as it is compulsions, no matter how small, with which I move forward as best I can. They spring up from a more hidden ego, as well as from deep fears and wounds that have crystallized in me throughout my life, driven by a secret desire for power. They stoke my impatience, often pushing me to act in haste. At other times, I don't want to do anything; I go in circles. Sometimes they prompt me to criticize certain people, to interrupt conversations to say what I know, what I think is right and true. I am still far from being "disarmed" in the sense that Patriarch Athenagoras invites us to be. I have a long way to go to freely avoid these compulsions. But how to overcome them? The best way is to lessen the power of fear. Learning to recognize the times when these fears awaken in me. I need more time, and silence. I need to do real work on myself to awaken my interiority and my small inner voice. My friends can help me. But I cannot do without personal prayer if I want the Holy Spirit to fulfill in me his work of love.

It is in recognizing that there are fears at the root of our compulsions that we can truly receive the gift of those who are oppressed. We must become more humble ourselves to become more free. Does not this encounter with the oppressed, and with everyone, have its source in the mutual love between Jesus, oppressed on the cross, and his Father?

25

From Generosity to Encounter

I remember a leader from a L'Arche community in Australia who came to see me. Before getting involved in L'Arche, she had accompanied with great generosity and skill young people who were trapped in prostitution. One night, as she was walking through a large park in Sydney, she found a man dying of an overdose. It was not the first time she had crossed paths with him. She took him in her arms. With his final breath, the man said to her, "You never wanted to meet me; you always wanted to change me." The woman was greatly shaken. It is not easy to encounter the other. It takes time. Or rather: you have to "waste" time to build mutual trust. This man had his story, a story that definitely included suffering. If we listen to the other's story, we start to cry together. We feel powerless before them. It takes time to help them discover the source of their life and rediscover confidence in what is best and most human in them.

This means moving from generosity to encounter. I would even go so far as to speak of a sacrament of encounter, a moment of grace. A human being who humbly encounters another human being: mutual presence, respectful listening that awakens life and one's self-confidence. But how can we free ourselves from our fears, our wounds, our feelings of superiority that hinder encounter? Doesn't this happen by discovering in ourselves the peace of God, this state of relaxation, of great openness, that renews our view of the other and allows us to listen to them with respect, for they also are a child of God?

Encounter implies a readiness to receive from the other. I know a man who was born into a perfect family. He was a brilliant student who made his parents proud. After graduation, he had a successful career, landing promotion after promotion. In the world's eyes, he was the ideal man. In the midst of all his activities, this man with boundless energy even found the time to help a few people who were in trouble. He was good at everything. Except for one thing: he was not able to listen to and encounter the oppressed, to enter into a real relationship with them. He was too focused on himself, on his own abilities, to be open to other people's weaknesses. It was in learning of his daughter's mental illness that this man began to change. In the face of her illness, he lost his footing. He felt overwhelmed. He had to accept his own poverty with humility. He had to learn to ask for help. In the end, it was his daughter who helped him to descend into the heart of his humanity, at the cost of a true encounter. He was transformed by his daughter's gift of life and her love.

*

In his testament, Saint Francis of Assisi reveals that for a long time he had had a sense of revulsion towards lepers. One day, driven by the Holy Spirit, he felt called to go to them and live with them. After being exposed to them, he spoke of feeling a new tenderness in his body and mind. In an authentic encounter, in the joy of communion that he experienced with them without doing anything for them, he was transformed. The walls of fear around his heart, which had kept him at a distance from these oppressed people, crumbled. He found new freedom and the joy of communion in living as a child of God among other children of God: his primal innocence resonated with theirs. How can we pass from revulsion and total indifference to a true encounter? At the social level, this can happen through recognition of the legitimacy of the lives of the most marginalized and the passing of laws to protect them. And then, at some point, comes movement towards fellowship: they are human, like me. That is when true generosity can be born: I want to help them, to support them materially. Finally, against all odds, I encounter one of them, I listen to them. We talk together. I am affected by their story. It's a heart-to-heart, a communion, that allows each of us to receive from the other.

In the image of Saint Francis of Assisi – Poverello, the little poor man – many men and women today feel unable to take this step, to cross the road that no one dares to cross. They have not found true inner freedom. So they desperately seek a situation that can help them feel secure and valued. Without this security, we feel lost when we meet those who are oppressed, like Pauline. We want to change them; we don't manage to encounter them. We cannot cross invisible borders alone. With our own weaknesses, we can, however, follow those who dared to do so thanks to a call from God and in community.

So, many young people come to L'Arche as volunteers to help us for a year. Some of them desperately lack confidence in themselves and have experienced failure, or have lacked love, support and encouragement in their families. In community, these assistants are gradually transformed as they discover that they are loved by those they came to help. The result is new strength, an inner freedom in them. They rediscover their self-confidence. The walls of fear gradually fall down. As messengers of peace, they find life and joy in a world filled with so much violence.

26

The Truth Springs Forth from Below

In 2004, the communities of L'Arche got involved in a process called "Identity and mission." This international-level reflection resulted in a definition that I think is wonderful: "L'Arche is the place of relationship that transforms and becomes a sign for the world." This is a small revolution! At the beginning, I saw L'Arche as being from God: the assistants who joined us were God's envoys. If they gradually discovered the true meaning of our mission, it was through a personal encounter with Jesus. Yet, the wording of our mission evolved from what I believed at the beginning. In community, we discovered and articulated what we were living: an experience with people who had a disability, who shaped and transformed us, humanized us and opened us to God. As if the truth flowed from the hearts of those who are deprived, those who are excluded from society, because of their intellectual disability. I felt torn between my initial vision of L'Arche – a mission within the Catholic Church – and the one that emerged through our development, and that seemed to me "more human." I gradually understood that this vision was part of God's plan, Word-made-flesh to become the brother of every human being. "Leaving home without knowing where we are going, because God is leading us ... stretching in hope towards the city to come, as witnesses of which the Letter to the Hebrews says, 'looking to Jesus the pioneer and perfecter of our faith' (Heb 11:1–12:2)."[2] People with a disability reveal God's presence in the most fragile and forsaken of our world. As Saint John Chrysostom wrote, they become sacrament, source of grace, presence of God. And Saint Vincent de Paul speaks of the poor being our teachers.

This truth springs forth from below, from an encounter, involving consequences on the ecumenical and interfaith level. If we encounter the other authentically – whatever their religion or lack of religion – we touch their identity as child of God, beyond all other affiliations. We reach them and encounter them in the deepest part of their being, in their radical humility, that is, what is most vulnerable, poor and good in them. In the place where their longing to be loved for who they are is expressed. At this level of encounter, each person can offer their spiritual fruitfulness, whatever name is given to God, who is One, the Father of all.

But how can we discover the treasure of the other if we have not discovered our own? This question pushed me, once again, to deepen my quest for truth. Descending and delving into my depths, in the hope of finding God there, hidden below the sediment of my life. What a long way we must go to become free!

＊

On this winding path, we are neither alone nor poor. The Word of God is a powerful leaven to fertilize our lives. The book of Isaiah has often enlightened me on this point. In chapter 58, the prophet asks this key question: What is the fast that God

---

2   Translation of the pastoral letter of the North African Bishops, 1977, quoted by Christian Salenson in his book *L'échelle mystique du dialogue de Christian de Chergé* (Bayard, 2016).

prefers? Is it when we deny ourselves and denigrate ourselves before him? Here is his response:

> Is not this the fast that I choose:
>> to loose the bonds of injustice,
>> to undo the thongs of the yoke,
> to let the oppressed go free,
>> and to break every yoke?
> Is it not to share your bread with the hungry,
>> and bring the homeless poor into your house;
> when you see the naked, to cover them,
>> and not to hide yourself from your own kin?
> Then your light shall break forth like the dawn,
>> and your healing shall spring up quickly;
> your vindicator shall go before you,
>> the glory of the Lord shall be your rearguard.
> Then you shall call, and the Lord will answer;
>> you shall cry for help, and he will say, Here I am.

If I encounter the poor with compassion and mercy, it is they who transform me. "Then your light shall break forth like the dawn...."

Jesus tells us that at the Last Judgment, the King will say to those on his right:

"Come, you that are blessed by my Father, inherit the kingdom prepared for you from the foundation of the world; for I was hungry and you gave me food, I was thirsty and you gave me something to drink, I was a stranger and you welcomed me, I was naked and you gave me clothing, I was sick and you took care of me, I was in prison and you visited me." Then the righteous will answer him, "Lord, when was it that we saw you hungry and gave you food, or thirsty and gave you something to drink? And when was it that we saw you a stranger and welcomed you, or naked and gave you clothing? And when was it that we saw you sick or in prison and visited you?" And the king will answer them, "Truly I tell you, just as you did it to one of the least of these who are members of my family, you did it to me." (Matthew 25:34-40)

To encounter someone who is poor and oppressed is to encounter Jesus.

Fr. Joseph Wresinski, founder of the movement Aide à toute détresse, better known as ATD Fourth World, told some L'Arche assistants: "The people with a disability whom you meet every day and who are the centre of your life have received the mission of rekindling love and spreading love, compelling men and women to love, to love themselves and be loved."

In the book of Leviticus, God tells the Israelites: "Be holy, for I the Lord your God am holy" (19:1-2). Jesus says, "Be merciful, just as your Father is merciful" (Luke 6:36). Being merciful, close to those who suffer, living with them, often involves getting your feet and hands dirty. In becoming closer to God, we gradually are transformed into men and women of goodness and compassion. And if we encounter with compassion those who are in the muck and cry out in suffering, we become like God. We live like God. We live in God. Together, we become builders of the kingdom, builders of peace.

27

"I Am Happy!"

Patrick and I have lived in the same home since 1981. He is 66 years old. We often eat at the same table. Patrick is a sensitive person. His childhood and adolescence were punctuated by stays in the hospital for children with mental illness in Perray-Vaucluse. We remember his father, Albert, now dead, as a wonderful man, very close to L'Arche. A former prisoner of war, he was active in the Communist Party. Patrick, because of his mental illness, cannot carry on a coherent conversation. He has true psychosis. He can't stop himself from dwelling on certain words or ideas, as if he were going in circles. But Patrick is well liked and appreciated for who he is. At meals, we often hear his inimitable laugh, and then he cries out, "I am happy! I am happy!" Sometimes, he throws himself on the floor, miming a revolver with his hand, acting out one of the fights he has seen in a Hollywood western or a James Bond film. We all laugh: he is joy personified. Patrick is fond of tobacco. Once a month, he and I go to a restaurant with Odile Ceyrac for dinner. During the meal, Patrick gets up suddenly and asks the person at the next table: "Do you smoke?" If the person says yes, Patrick quickly replies: "Do you have a cigarette for me?" Ah, Patrick loves a celebration. He loves to dance. He likes good food. And bread, bread and more bread… When he goes to mass, he always wears the same hat, or sometimes a cap. With my legalistic upbringing, I can't stop myself from suggesting that he remove his hat before the celebration. Patrick is good. He follows my recommendation for a few seconds, then puts his hat back on. Patrick is who he is. He is happy, although he has many anxieties: "I will die someday. But I'm not ready. I can wait." Yes, Patrick. You can wait. At times, in the living room of our home at Val fleuri, we sit side by side. He places his hand on mine. We sit in silence. A moment of communion. He knows he is loved. It's a great mystery: Patrick evangelizes me.

28

She Watches over Me

Annicette is 66. She arrived at L'Arche when she was 18, a damaged young woman. Early in her life, she was taken away from her parents, who were alcoholics. Bounced around from one foster family to another, she suffered a lot. She was then placed in a home run by nuns. There, too, Annicette did not feel known and loved. L'Arche was a turning point in her life. One day, as we shared a meal, she started talking to me about the orphans in Haiti who were waiting for families to adopt them, after the earthquake that hit the island in 2010. She said to me: "Everything possible should be done so they are given a home with good and loving families." This observation touched me: "Annicette, are you speaking of yourself, of your experience and your suffering?" "Yes," she said. At Val, as I saw with my own eyes, she became increasingly happy. She loved the others and couldn't help embracing them. Everyone loves her. Annicette has a little doll she is fond of. She takes great care of it. You can tell that this helps her maintain her equilibrium. I must say that Annicette is gentle and kind to me.

Her mother's heart is expressed particularly in the way she asks about my health: "Have you taken your pills?" When I go out, she helps me by handing me my coat. And the advice she gives me is always wise: "Don't tire yourself out; you need to rest." Annicette has truly found a family. I am so happy to live with her. I think she needs me, as a kind of father figure. I need her, too. And like her, I have found a family.

André, whom we like to call Doudoul, is a friend I have lived with for a long time. He is 65, an affectionate man who loves to give and to receive. This craving for affection explains the rough and difficult aspect of his personality. Doudoul has issues with authority, especially with men. One day, he went to see a cardiologist. When he got back, as we were having a meal, we asked him how his doctor's appointment went.

"Very well."

"What did he see in your heart?"

"Jesus," replied Doudoul, as if it were obvious.

"And what is Jesus doing in your heart?"

"He's resting."

Doudoul, who loves going to mass often, knows that Jesus lives in him.

29

Drawn to a Holy Spring

Recently, around 40 members of our community made a pilgrimage to Lisieux, in France. It was a joy-filled journey that I was able to join. Once we got there, we stayed near the Carmelite convent. Nothing could put a damper on our joy. Patrick and André, two members of Val fleuri, were with us. I also saw Loïc and other friends from Les Fougères. The magic of such a pilgrimage is based on simple things: joy, prayer, laughter and sharing. We took advantage of this trip to Normandy to go and see the ocean. There, Patrick "swam," as he called it – that is, he took off his shoes and socks and waded along the water's edge. This brief time with little Thérèse of Lisieux was important for me and for everyone. She had described her convent as "My little holy Ark." In walking in her footsteps, I rediscovered the mystery of Thérèse, her little way, her total trust in Jesus and in his love. Living each day doing small things with great love: what a treasure! Early on, her experience nurtured my life in community. Thérèse mentioned, for example, the sister who was always so mean to her, but to whom, in spite of everything, Thérèse gave her brightest smile. There are deep bonds between Thérèse and L'Arche. My grandmother, also named Thérèse, had the same spiritual director as the saint of Lisieux: Fr. Pichon. When this Jesuit priest wrote to my grandmother, he often spoke of his "two little Thérèses."

A pilgrimage is always an incredible time that highlights the pilgrimage of our life, the stages that mark its winding course. We are always drawn to a spring. A holy spring. Seeing Lisieux again injected me with new strength. Here, a young woman, dead by age 24, was chosen by God to lead a true revolution in the Church: learning to love Jesus simply, with trust.

The Carmelites, scattered across the globe, are an extraordinary source of life. We need these silent monks and nuns, as we need all those who watch over us in prayer, sometimes outside of monasteries. When I get up early in the morning, I like to recall that they are gathered in prayer at the same time. I unite myself with them in the heart of God.

30

What I Owe to John Paul II

During my L'Arche journey, John Paul II often supported me. It all started rather mysteriously. In the 1980s, I met the Polish pope regularly… in my dreams. In these dreams, I tried to approach him, to speak to him. I didn't have to wait long for this connection to take a more rational path. During these same years, I travelled to Krakow to support the starting of a L'Arche community with help from the Little Sisters of Jesus. During this time on Karol Wojtyła's home turf, I met a Polish priest, a close friend of the pope's. Thus, in 1987, a delegation from L'Arche was invited to an audience at the Vatican. During this gathering, John Paul II motioned to me: he wanted to meet me. After a private mass in his little chapel, he invited me to have breakfast at his table, away from the stiffness of protocol. Besides his secretary, Stanisław Dziwisz – future bishop of Krakow – and another priest of his entourage, I was the only guest. The pope let me speak. I told him with passion about my encounter with people with a disability, and the founding of L'Arche. I remember telling him in detail about our friend Éric, whom we welcomed after he left the psychiatric hospital. Deaf and blind, Éric could barely walk. Like many, he had been abandoned by his family and experienced terrible anguish. John Paul II listened closely, although they told me later he had not really seen how Éric could do me any good, or how living with him had changed me. During this conversation, I told him I had often dreamed about him, saying that since he had visited my subconscious, he was clearly like a father to me.

After this conversation, I started receiving many invitations to Rome. In 1987, I was invited to the synod of bishops on the vocation and mission of the laity in the Church and in the world. Then there was a large gathering of new communities in St. Peter's Square. Chiara Lubich, founder of Focolari, Don Luigi Giussani, founder of Communion and Liberation, Kiko Argüello, founder of The Neocatechumenal Way, and I each outlined the missions of our communities in the pope's presence. To be honest, I was rather surprised to find myself on the stage with these other founders, as L'Arche seemed so small to me – and will remain so, in my eyes. With simplicity, I once again told the story of Éric, who had transformed me from within. And I reminded John Paul II that he was in our prayers.

There were many other meetings in Rome during his pontificate. To mark the jubilee of the year 2000, theologians from around the world travelled to the city to assess theological advances since the Council. I was invited to share my perspective on L'Arche, one of the fruits of Vatican II, to this gathering of experts. Not long after this, I spoke at a Eucharistic Congress at the Pontifical Lateran University. Then, in 2004, the pope convened an international symposium on the dignity and rights of the mentally disabled person, which I attended with 15 other people. The pope shared with us this wonderful message: "It is said, justifiably so, that disabled people are humanity's privileged witnesses. They can teach everyone about the love that saves us; they can become heralds of a new world, no longer dominated by force, violence and aggression, but by love, solidarity and acceptance, a new world transfigured by the light of Christ, the Son of God who became incarnate, who was crucified and rose for us."

A high point of our friendship was John Paul II's visit to Lourdes in August 2004; it will remain an unforgettable moment – our last real conversation, before illness would overtake him the following year. The bishop of Tarbes and Lourdes, Bishop Jacques Perrier, asked me to lead a walking meditation on the mysteries of light of the rosary, with the pope in attendance. He was very weak; he followed me slowly, seated in his popemobile. I walked about 10 metres ahead of him, stopping for each new mystery. I used simple words that spoke to all. Each meditation lasted for three or four minutes. As I reflected on Jesus proclaiming the Good News to the poor, just a few steps separated me from the pope. We looked each other straight in the eye for a long time. In front of this weakened and tested person, the Gospels suddenly came to life in a searing truth. Jesus, I said, came to proclaim the Good News to us. Our pope is poor. And he is proclaiming the Good News in his poverty. He is showing the world that God is present in weakness. I continued to look right at him, so near to his broken body. When the procession had finally dispersed, he motioned to me to come and sit beside him. Then he slipped his rosary into the palm of my hand. This communion with John Paul II impressed me deeply. Nearly 50 years earlier, I had been pushed out of L'Eau vive by representatives of the Holy Office. I had felt rejected by the Church that I desired to serve with all my being. Through our meetings, the future Saint John Paul II bandaged my wounds, confirming in the best possible ways the path of L'Arche. Years later, I can still feel his presence. The presence of a father. A friend... a friend to whom I owe a new freedom of my heart. A friend who continues to watch over L'Arche.

31

The Fear that the Messenger
Overshadows the Message

From 1956 to 1964, I experienced years of calm, peace and solitude. Happy to live with Jesus. Working on my philosophy dissertation. Filled with the desire to succeed in my studies. I was, I believe, a fulfilled and even a satisfied man. I confidently awaited signs from God. The success of my teaching at the University of Toronto was my first experience of notoriety. But it didn't last. The origins of L'Arche seemed like a natural follow-up to my chosen solitude. My model was the hidden life of Jesus in Nazareth. A simple life in community. Cooking and manual labour. Poor among the poor. Some might politely see me as a friendly visionary. What was this 36-year-old man – and what's more, a bachelor – playing at, insisting on living with people with severe disabilities? Outside of Dr. Léone Richet and a few other doctors, specialists from the Clermont psychiatric hospital saw me as a mystic corrupted by Christian views. They sized me up from above. In their eyes, our venture lacked professionalism. Recognition happened step by step, discreetly. When Édouard Balladur was prime minister, his wife, Marie-Josèphe, came to visit us. She left amazed at the way of life in L'Arche homes. Our joy touched her heart. She soon suggested to her influential husband that I be awarded the Legion of Honour. Little by little, others began to see in our shared way of life, our radical simplicity, a form of revelation. L'Arche, able to heal the weakest among us, became a place of transformation through friendship and life together.

✳

March 2015. I found out that I would be the next recipient of the Templeton Prize, on behalf of a foundation created 28 years earlier by a renowned North American philanthropist. When it comes to social engagement, this honour is one of the greatest in the world. Mother Teresa, Brother Roger, Desmond Tutu and the Dalai Lama have all received it. But why me? The foundation, as the official news release stated, wanted to highlight my innovative discoveries on the central role of vulnerable people in the search for a more just, more inclusive and more humane society. This tribute warmed my heart. And of course, it was a wonderful, even unhoped for, moment in the spotlight for L'Arche.

And yet I was ambivalent about this sudden resurgence of fame. I worried that the public would be too interested in the messenger and not in his message. The message of L'Arche, like that of Faith and Light, is a simple one. If we agree to live with people with intellectual disabilities, we will be transformed. Although they are poor on an intellectual level, they teach us to become more human, more authentic and therefore more engaged in works of peace. On this essential condition: that we agree to enter into relationship with them.

Personally, I was not unmoved to be honoured by the Templeton Foundation. And I am fully aware of the danger facing those who bask in honours. Pride is always lurking. In the truth of my being, I know that L'Arche is the work of God.

I am forced to recognize it. Yes, God chose me to start this movement. But I am always mindful of my frailties and my weaknesses, which can cause harm. That is always with me, as is the suffering in the face of the injuries committed within L'Arche by Fr. Thomas. However, in my heart of hearts, I am happy that the message of L'Arche and of Faith and Light is now being promoted throughout the world. People with an intellectual disability are better known, better acknowledged. They finally enjoy a greater place within the Church and, I dare to believe, in our societies.

32

Saint John and the Gospel of Freedom

He is "the disciple Jesus loved." My life in L'Arche made me go deeper into, and I dare say better understand, the Gospel of John. He has given us a burning and unique word. Before taking this path, I already loved this Gospel. Why? I think that Saint John reveals a path to us. A path to better understand Jesus and live with him. One of this text's key points is found in the Greek word *menein*, which means "stay." It all begins with two disciples who, after leaving John the Baptist, follow Jesus. "What are you looking for?" he asks them. "Rabbi, where are you staying?" they reply. This is the secret: the Gospel of John allows us to gradually discover where Jesus is staying. Of course, he stays in the Father. Of course, he stays in the Church. But over time, in meditating on John's words, we discover that he lives in each one of us. The entire Gospel seeks to help us become friends of Jesus. The heart of the Gospel is friendship. And this is also the meaning of L'Arche. Encountering people with an intellectual disability, living in communion with them, becoming their friend, and staying with them… The Gospel of John taught me – but I feel that I must, again and again, deepen it – to simply stay with Jesus, to find him in the poor and the vulnerable.

The heart of the Gospel is this word of Jesus: "Live in my love." If we live in Jesus, our heart opens to all people. Those we feel close to and those who seem like enemies. That is a given, because John wrote that God so loved the world that he sent his only Son to give life. The Gospel of John is a Gospel of life and of peace. "Peace I leave with you; my peace I give to you. I do not give to you as the world gives" (John 14:27). Jesus gives us this peace in helping us discover that the key involves staying with him, living with him. And letting him live in us. If I live in him and he in me, I can love others as Jesus loves them. And Jesus loves them in teaching us to go down, to get on our knees, to wash other people's feet. Not commanding them from above. Not trying to gain the upper hand. Jesus washes the disciples' feet and says, "Do you know what I have done to you? You call me Teacher and Lord – and you are right, for that is what I am. So if I, your Lord and Teacher, have washed your feet, you also ought to wash one another's feet" (John 13:12-14).

This is the centre and heart of L'Arche: being there to humbly serve the poorest, to lift them up so they can take their rightful place in the Church and in societies. And so they can help us to receive the truth of our own poverty.

But the disciples experienced the washing of the feet as a moment of crisis. Peter refuses to participate: "You will never wash my feet." He believed in a powerful Jesus, who would free the people from the yoke of the Romans. Yet the master lowers himself like a slave, on his knees. Later, this same Peter would cry, "I do not know the man!" In fact, he did not know a weak Jesus, letting himself be pushed around by the Jewish and Roman authorities. Jesus, in becoming weak, reveals to us the role of weakness as the place of relationship and mutual aid, as a place of encounter with God. "My power is made perfect in weakness," he would say to Paul (2 Corinthians 12:9).

In Northern Ireland, which at the time was gripped by a violent conflict between Unionists (mostly Protestants) and nationalists (mostly Catholics), I had the great joy of speaking about the washing of feet during a day of prayer and reflection for the leaders of different Christian communities (Catholic Church, Church of Ireland, Presbyterian, Methodist, Salvation Army...). At the end, we washed each other's feet. It was an intense moment. A few years later, I was invited to the Ecumenical Centre in Geneva to preach to 180 representatives of different churches. During the final celebration, we once again did the washing of feet. It was so moving to see an Orthodox bishop wash the feet of a black woman, an American pastor. During this kind of ecumenical encounter, we cannot always share Communion at the same Eucharistic table, because of our divisions. But we can bend down to wash each other's feet. And so we live unity in humility and poverty.

Saint John showed me a Jesus who cared about unity. Jesus died so that all people can come together. Peace, which so many of us desire, is born of unity. At Jacob's well, Jesus met a wounded woman. She was a Samaritan, despised because of who she was. But Jesus promised to give her living water, a new life – that is, his holy Spirit. Although she was so poor, she was transformed. In her turn, she would bring other Samaritans to Jesus. Once again, Jesus acts through the poor. Thanks to Saint John, we know that "Those who love me will keep my word, and my Father will love them, and we will come to them and make our home with them" (John 14:23). Living in Jesus so he lives in us, and so we can go to the most in need, to receive a source of living water and reveal their value to them.

33

The Evolution of Humanity: Towards Greater Unity

Saint John, at the beginning of his Gospel, says that the Word of God created all. "All things came into being through him, and without him not one thing came into being." Our universe, with its planets and galaxies, is incredibly beautiful. It is a unified whole. This is also true of our Earth and living beings: each one needs the others. The tiniest insects and the largest animals have their own place and their own mission. With the arrival of human beings, disorder entered the world. Instead of cultivating the Earth and improving it, they began to destroy its unity by polluting the water and the air, and wiping out species. Over time, humans evolved. There were more of them. They often sought unity with others through force and domination, through power and greed, through doing away with the weakest people and groups. Today, with technological advances, with the fear and hate that separate groups and countries, a question arises: Are we moving towards the destruction of humanity, or is peace among people possible? Is a path to unity opening up? Reconciliation between human beings is inevitable, even if it is sometimes painful. If we look closely, we notice, however, that this evolution began amid great poverty, among small, scattered groups that, little by little, got together. I see in this an essential sign to shed light on our current situation. Will our world move towards peace or towards more violence and war?

In 1978, I had the opportunity to take a long trip to Papua New Guinea, an island in the southeast Pacific Ocean. The country had just achieved independence and was being born before our eyes. When I got there, they told me that more than 734 languages still coexisted on the island. Some dialects were becoming extinct, while others remained vibrant. This diversity fascinated me. When I met people, instead of giving me the name of their village, they identified themselves by saying "my talk" – in other words, "my language." For me, coming from Europe, this was amazing. It was like discovering the former face of our civilization. I observed Papua New Guinea, with its mountains and forests, its small groups that were starting to expand, thinking beyond the borders of their ancestors. They no longer hesitated, in order to feed themselves and make a living, to cross the mountains and forests, to find new places to settle. In this way, new groups formed, each with its own language, culture, way of worshipping God, marriage customs, relationship to medicine… Over time, a new country was forged. A world took shape, through all these small groups, through encounters and intermarrying. What I saw in this emerging country helped me understand the basic shift that has allowed our societies to evolve and grow.

＊

How was our world built? Over time, human beings, with new techniques, scattered further and further to conquer new lands. The bravest dared to board creaky vessels, then bigger ones, to cross the oceans. Gradually, clans and tribes formed nations. These nations started to do battle with new weapons.

Trade expanded, and with it a spirit of competition; cultures were intermingled. The world grew, but new groups that formed were plagued by rivalries, desires for domination and conquest. Great kings and warlords led the peoples. All you need to do is stroll around the Arc de Triomphe, in the heart of Paris, to recall that many of them still haunt our memories: memories of an expanding world that seeks to be made one based on relationships of violence and confrontation.

*

The major religions thrived during this troubled history. Buddhism, Hinduism, Confucianism, Judaism, Christianity, Islam… Each found its place, certain that it possessed the truth. Like others, Christians thought they must convert their peers to offer them ultimate knowledge of the divine and the human. Even today, many believers think that acceptance of their faith is an essential prerequisite to be saved. They must convert others. The human journey is beset with religious wars, from Medieval crusades to current conflicts in Africa or the Middle East.

*

However, two recent events in the history of Catholicism seem to me to indicate a turning point towards a new understanding of human relationships. First, the Second Vatican Council (1962–1965), whose pastoral constitution *Gaudium et spes* affirms that personal conscience is "the most secret core and sanctuary of a man. There he is alone with God, Whose voice echoes in his depths" (no. 16). This conscience is given to each human being to lead them to what is good, what is just, what is true. Second, the bold encounter in Assisi, convened in 1986 by John Paul II. Religious leaders from across the spectrum dared to do something unprecedented aimed at a new path to peace: dialogue.

Essentially, this is the big question. It's the only urgent question we need to ask: Where is peace found? How can we achieve it? It took three terrible wars between France and Germany for European construction to begin. The foreboding that in the era of atomic weapons, our age-old rivalries would become suicidal. Following the Second World War, the Universal Declaration of Human Rights adopted by the United Nations emphasized that the recognition of the inherent dignity of each person in the human family is the foundation of freedom, justice and peace in the world. Gradually, groups began to become aware that each person deserved consideration. Discourse on the Indigenous peoples of Canada, at the beginning of the 21st century, evolved. Before then, children were forcibly separated from their families, language and culture to become "real" Canadians. Now we honour Indigenous people, with their love for the earth and for nature. In the same way, Westerners no longer consider Africans as savages to be civilized. We now recognize the wisdom of their civilizations. I could give many other examples. Gradually, we started speaking about people with a disability with more respect, and the same for people who are homosexual – who, even 50 years ago, were considered criminals. We started to realize that, beyond affiliations, cultures and religions, each human being is important.

Beyond all the fears, all the wars and the hatred that is widespread throughout the world, and beyond the greed that harms our planet, thousands upon thousands of small lights are shining: lights of peace and life through which each person, whatever their culture, their abilities or their disabilities, is seen as precious. Peace is thus not only the work of soldiers, politicians and economists, but is the responsibility of everyone. "Ultimately, we have just one moral duty: to reclaim large areas of peace in ourselves, more and more peace, and to reflect it toward others. And the more peace there is in us, the more peace there will also be in our troubled world," writes Etty Hillesum in her journal. A new world is beginning to appear on the horizon, which depends on each of us and on the transformation of our hearts. This vision of universal peace, linked to the inner freedom and growth of each person, can be supported by new communications if we use them wisely: smartphones, Facebook, Twitter, etc. We can now communicate to encourage each other to become more free, more real, more open to the action of the Holy Spirit. Thank God, the group is no longer a synonym for imprisonment. It is also the place where we draw strength to go to encounter those who are marginalized or different. Where we help each other become men and women of peace, small communities of light, "in which [we] shine like stars in the world," as Saint Paul said (Philippians 2:15). These communities are not straitjackets that imprison us in our clans and our certainties of belonging to a group that holds the only truth. It was with great joy that I found the statement of Benedict XVI, before his humble and simple act of giving up the office of pope: "The truth is not possessed by anyone." He wrote this for the Middle East, where so many religions live together. What a message from this pope who was always fond of L'Arche!

It is not merely a question of dialogue, but also of encountering those who are different from us. Fr. Joseph Wresinski goes so far as to say that unity will not be possible until we realize that it goes through the poorest, as the deepest division is the one that exists between the more affluent and those who are left behind. Who better than the disadvantaged can know, through having experienced it in the flesh, how destructive human oppression is? If we listen to these communities formed with the marginalized and the oppressed, their experience teaches us the true meaning of justice and freedom. Yes, a new world is taking shape, in which each person is invited to be a messenger of peace by becoming the friend of someone who is marginalized and rejected. This friendship will transform both of them. This world for which Jesus, the Prince of Peace, prayed, "that they may all be one. As you, Father, are in me and I am in you, may they also be in us" (John 17:21) – he who died to "gather into one all the dispersed children of God" (John 11:52). It is not always easy to find yourself between what was and what must come. This place is called hope. Hope that is hidden in the poor: hope for peace.

The brothers of Taizé, who work with street children in Bangladesh and who were very involved in the founding of L'Arche there, wrote in one of their letters: "The challenge we face today pushes us to show that service given to our brothers and sisters who are weak and vulnerable indicates the opening up of a path of peace and unity: welcoming everyone in the rich diversity of religions and cultures, and serving the poor, prepares a future of peace." When we encounter each other with a view to mission for the poor and the weak, a special unity is forged. It is forged by life. Yes, let us all stand together for peace.

34

The Mystery of the Person

D oes this evolution of the world not correspond to an
evolution in the notion and value of the human person?
For centuries, the person was measured by their abilities, their
qualities, their role in society; based on this logic, the weak
could not find their place. People felt superior on the basis of
their knowledge, their status. In this world, women, the poor,
slaves and people with a disability didn't count. Jesus certainly
focused on the person by choosing "the weak and the foolish."
But from age to age, universal consciousness sided with power,
skill and performance, which were seen as the building blocks
of human identity – at the risk of denying the share of weakness
and vulnerability inherent in each of us. The end of the Second
World War, in 1945, with the discovery of Auschwitz and the
ravages of the atomic bomb, encouraged the realization that all
people have value, with their freedom and their uniqueness.
That is the meaning of the Universal Declaration of Human
Rights, enacted by the United Nations in 1948: "All human
beings are born free and equal in dignity and rights. They are
endowed with reason and conscience and should act towards
one another in a spirit of brotherhood." Gradually, humanity
understood that beyond the quest for power, each person's life
mattered, in its most intimate and personal aspects. That is
where their treasure lies. We begin to recognize that the person

holds a mystery. Can we define the person? No, it's impossible, or we will imprison their mystery with a label. The innocence at the beginning of life is perhaps the best key to understanding this concept. Even tarnished by fears, violence and the losses we experience, this innocence never dies. At the heart of our lives, isn't it our original weakness that makes us run towards what is new and urges us to push the boundaries? We are never completely satisfied. Our heart craves knowledge, power, wealth, love, more and always more, indefinitely, while hidden in the depths of our hearts is an emptiness, a searching for the infinite, a desire for God. This emptiness is our greatest wealth, but also our greatest weakness. Human beings feel they are being dragged towards an unknown future, one that they hope will be better than the present. Unlike us, the animal world remains set in its natural order. There is no new future for it, beyond the continuity of the species. What constitutes the person is instead this deep awareness of belonging to the human family – whether we choose to serve and honour it or not. Even today, the smile of an innocent child, simple and pure, best reveals to me the mystery of the person. Each person is a mystery for receiving God; each person is an immense weakness waiting for God. The mystery of the person is the encounter.

35

Working for a More Humane Society

For a long time after I left the Navy, I tended to spiritualize many aspects of my daily life. I wanted to remain in prayer, to continue the work of interiority. I was barely interested in the world's problems. I didn't seek to love others as Jesus loves them – Jesus, "the man" par excellence (John 19:5). It was at L'Arche that I discovered the importance of each person in their humanity – especially the most marginalized. It was not about converting others but understanding them, encountering them, creating links of trust. Listening to them, and doing so humbly. The major problem of our times reflects the dehumanization of our societies. So many young people dive into a fierce quest for personal success, without a shared vision, or fall victim to discouragement or boredom with no hope in the future. They ease their sadness and their fear of the void with drugs, alcohol or other addictions. The political world is in a shambles, with each party consumed by internal conflicts. Our churches struggle to find the hope and simplicity of the Gospel. Some Christians fall into a narrow form of protecting the faith. Happily, amid this turmoil, Pope Francis offers a message of peace. A message that he sends us to take to all the fringes of our societies. He encourages us to encounter and lift up those who are rejected to lead them towards hope. I used to think that being a humanist meant rejecting faith and spirituality. I gradually understood that, on the contrary, it involves becoming more human, placing spirituality at the heart of our selves. This involves the belief that together we all make up a big family. A universal place, open to the other and especially to the poorest, to meet them in what is most beautiful and most vulnerable in them. The period we are in expresses a need that is crying out to be humanized. Businesses, hospitals, schools, institutions, universities and the churches are called to become places where each person finds their place, where each person is seen as important and is heard – beginning with the weakest and the most marginalized, for they are the ones who open the way of true humanization. Not places of domination by the strong, where idols like money and power reign: these, which demand so much from victims so that they can survive, dehumanize those who worship them. But places where relationships come first, places where performance and knowledge have not become master. Places where all work together so that the churches' Gospel mission is not hindered by the institution.

We must go beyond what can seem negative in the other, in the one who is different from us. We must learn to recognize what is good and positive in each person. The danger would be to stick with competition, in the position of the victors, rather than supporting solidarity. Yes, let us acknowledge the gift hidden in the other, in the one who is different: their primal innocence. Let us receive this gift, emphasizing fellowship over domination, community over individualism. This means exploring what one needs to become oneself and to discover one's deepest heart. Free to grow in the love of others. This often comes through silent prayer. It also comes through community. People united in humility and in truth around a shared mission.

36

From Ireland to Palestine,
a Path of Peace

In the 1990s, US President Bill Clinton sent Senator George Mitchell to facilitate the peace process in Northern Ireland. Mitchell conducted the negotiations between the different parties of this intractable and bloody conflict with intelligence and patience. He quickly understood that his mission would be doomed to fail if no one changed their attitude. They constantly pinned the blame on each other. Dreams of peace became more elusive every day. The senator then had a surprising idea: one evening, he invited all the participants to a restaurant in Belfast. The only rule was this: no talking politics at the table. They could speak only about themselves, their spouse, their children, rain and fine weather, what they were reading, and fishing... Things about being human. Everyone went along with it. It was the day after this gathering, on April 10, 1998, that they were able to sign the Good Friday Agreement, outlining a political solution to end three decades of violence and division. Of course, this momentum didn't last. But for one evening, Senator Mitchell brought things back to the essentials. Before becoming enemies, they were all human beings with a heart.

*

Another story about humanization is told by the South African Anglican bishop Desmond Tutu in *The Book of Forgiving*, which he wrote with his daughter. In it, the 1984 Nobel Peace Prize laureate tells the story of Bassam. At the age of 12, this young Palestinian saw one of his friends, the same age as him, die after being shot by an Israeli soldier. Bassam felt consumed by such a desire for vengeance that he started planning an attack against some Tsahal soldiers. After being arrested when he was 17, he was sentenced to seven years in prison. This only served to fan his hatred: he was beaten and oppressed. Insults flowed between the Israeli guards and the Palestinian prisoners. The atmosphere was harsh. But one encounter would change everything. Here is what Tutu writes:

> While in prison, Bassam engaged in a dialogue with his Israeli guard. Each thought the other was the "terrorist" and each equally denied being the "settler" in the land they shared. Through their conversations, they realized how much they had in common with the other. For Bassam, it was the first time he recalls feeling empathy in his life.

Tutu continues:

> Seeing the transformation that took place between him and his captor, as they recognized their shared humanity, Bassam realized that violence could never bring peace. This realization changed his life.[3]

These two stories offer us the same truth. Violence breeds violence. Only the discovery of our fragile humanity can open

---

3   Desmond Tutu and Mpho Andrea Tutu, *The Book of Forgiving: The Fourfold Path for Healing Ourselves and Our World* (HarperCollins, 2014).

a way to peace. How can I reach the other, who is different from me, and hear them in their vulnerability? Something has to change in me. This change of approach involves an open spirituality, oriented towards love and unconditional acceptance – the only way to receive the gift of the other.

However, this journey towards total freedom is anything but a long, quiet river. It is a path of suffering that calls for a profound transformation. Two women, one Israeli and one Palestinian, experienced the same tragedy: a son killed by the enemy.[4] The encounter of these two mothers, each one feeling the pain in her own flesh, must have had its extremely difficult moments. The enemy becoming a friend calls for a strength that breaks through and lifts us up. A strength that comes from God. These two women, each in her own way, rose above not only hatred for the enemy, but also the anger of their own group, who saw in their collaboration a betrayal of the cause. A cause that is often driven by violence; a quest for power. A path to peace calls for courage. It springs from the tears and suffering that we share.

---

4   *Nos larmes ont la même couleur* [Our Tears Are the Same Colour], Bushra Awad and Robi Damelin, with Anne Guion (Cherche-Midi, 2015).

37

A Few *Fioretti*

Throughout my life, I have received the immense grace to be called to proclaim the Gospel in many different contexts. Over and over, I have given witness that people with an intellectual disability are a privileged path to God. Everywhere I went, these words gave rise to moving encounters – disturbing at times, but always remarkable. They traced a path of hope and unity.

Ecumenism of the gulag

Soon after the fall of the Berlin Wall and the collapse of the Soviet system, I was invited to a Moscow theatre to give a retreat to Orthodox, Catholics, Baptists, Pentecostals... After a while, the official from the Pentecostal church got up and said, "In prison, we were all very united. Catholics, Orthodox, Pentecostals, Baptists. But now that we are free again, the issue of our divisions has broken out again."

My friend the mufti

In Syria, I gave a talk hosted by the mufti of Aleppo, who was considered a high Muslim official in his country. The auditorium was filled with 200 to 300 Muslims, mostly women. At the end of the gathering, the mufti got up and thanked me, saying, "If I have understood properly, you are telling us that if we stay close to people with an intellectual disability, they will lead us to God." Then he took me into an adjoining room, where we could have something to eat. He carefully picked up a small pastry and placed it in my mouth, a sign of special friendship between us.

A missed appointment...

A change of scene: now we are at the prestigious University of Notre Dame in the US, where L'Arche received a $10,000 donation during a ceremony. I had prepared a speech to be given to a large number of students. I had carefully crafted each phrase, wanting to encourage all these young Catholics to bring a message of hope to the poor of the world. They brought me to the auditorium: to my surprise, the audience was made up of around 50 men and women with severe disabilities, in wheelchairs, who came specially from a centre near the university. There were a few professors, but not a single student. I was amazed and bewildered. I left Notre Dame encouraged and moved, but sad and a little angry, like after a missed appointment: I had hoped to pass the torch to these young university students, the builders of tomorrow.

In the glow of a candle

In Calcutta I was the guest of Ramakrishna Centre, founded in memory of a great Hindu spiritual teacher. All the members of our local community were there, but few others, unfortunately. It felt strange; our little group in such a huge room. After about 15 minutes, the lights went out: a power outage. The other members of the audience took advantage of the blackout to tiptoe out of the room. After lighting a candle, I invited our members to form a circle around me. Of course,

I was disappointed in the lack of interest in our presence, but, in the chiaroscuro of the moment, we had an experience of unity.

Painful unity

One of the best presentations I can remember took place at the United Church of Canada's General Assembly, in close cooperation with L'Arche. How moving to see our witness received with such intensity and listening! Soon after, we had an ecumenical retreat with Catholic and Anglican bishops, as well as moderators from the United Church. I remember the pain many felt when we could not share Communion at the same table, despite the spiritual unity we had experienced.

Indigenous people of the Far North

In Canada's Far North, not far from Alberta, I had the joy of meeting representatives of the Dene, one of Canada's Indigenous peoples. None of them spoke French or English, so we communicated through an interpreter. Before the retreat began, a group from another Indigenous nation came to ask if I would come and preach to them the following year. But first, they wanted to make sure that I was speaking authentically: "Our elders will listen to you, and they will know if you are speaking the truth, for they will have dreams." I must have passed the test, because they confirmed at the end of the retreat that they would like to have me come to talk to them.

The moon between the bars...

Giving talks in large Canadian prisons, including high-security prisons, was one of my most radical experiences. In one of these, I had my own cell. With my eyes fixed on the moon, which was shining between the metal bars, I felt at one with all the prisoners who, in all the prisons in the world, were gazing at the sky at the same moment…

Thanks to our contacts in the prison system, we organized a weekend of reflection with inmates, guards and prison directors, but also chaplains. We were all staying in Ottawa, in a former prison. Everyone had their own cell. In the morning, we ate breakfast together. We didn't know each other. We went only by our first names: Jean, Pierre, Albert… So you didn't know if you were talking to a prison director, psychologist, guard or inmate. I quickly noticed that we were instinctively trying to figure out the other person's role, before even thinking of listening to them. But everyone played the game. Imagine our emotion, at the end of those two cloistered days, when each person could reveal who they were…

Serving on our knees

In one of our communities, a Muslim woman was reluctant to celebrate Holy Thursday with us. She thought this Christian ceremony was forbidden to her. Unable to accept that a man would wash her feet, and not being able to imagine washing his, she finally decided to join us as long as she was surrounded by women. She washed the feet of one of our members. And this touched something in her. At the end of the celebration, she said: "That's not a Christian ceremony, that's a ceremony for everyone." And she added, "From now on, I want to serve people on my knees."

38

Fr. Joseph Wresinski, Apostle of Transformation

I have already mentioned his name a couple of times in this book. I had the great privilege of knowing Fr. Joseph Wresinski (1917–1988), founder of ATD Fourth World. This remarkable man had himself grown up in extreme poverty, and over the many years he spent in Noisy-le-Grand, near Paris, he gave himself body and soul to people living in dire poverty. Fr. Joseph came to lead a reflection day in Trosly for assistants, on the Eucharist as a source of life for the marginalized. He also sent two of his best members to help in our community of Ouagadougou, in Burkina Faso, which was going through a difficult time. In addition to supporting the community, these two members of ATD helped me to find a centre that welcomed a large number of elderly women who had been banned from their homes and village, and to visit an overnight shelter for beggars in Ouagadougou and speak to the people. There were around 40 of them, in extreme poverty; each one had visible sores and physical disabilities, and was lying on the straw. What could I say to them? I felt lost. Jesus inspired me to tell them the parable of Lazarus (Luke 16:19-31): A beggar, covered in sores, was squatting before the house of a rich man, who hosted big parties. Lazarus would have loved to eat the crumbs that fell from the rich man's table. Lazarus died and, Jesus tells us, entered the bosom of Abraham. The rich man also died, but he went to the place of torment. He cried out to Abraham: "Send Lazarus to me, so he can cool my tongue with water." "Impossible," Abraham replied. "There is a chasm between you." I would say that Abraham could have added that this chasm already existed between them on earth when, from his house, the rich man never wanted to encounter Lazarus. This chasm is like the road that no one dares to cross near Santiago, in Chile – the road that separates the rich from the poor. The homeless people in the centre in Ouagadougou clapped at the end of the story, seeing Lazarus happy in the bosom of Abraham. Wasn't this the heart of their hopes? Fr. Joseph is a light for me. He says that "unity and peace cannot come unless we overcome the chasms that separate people." The person with a disability that you encounter every day, he told the assistants at L'Arche, is "a builder of the kingdom, because they are a builder of tenderness. They are a call for tenderness. They are a builder of the kingdom because they need to be loved, and they need to love." For him, the marginalized are the saviours of humanity.

39

Two Lights for My Path

Besides Mother Teresa, of whom I have already written, other women who were close to the poor and close to people of other religions have illuminated my life. They confirmed for me that my path of liberation and of seeker for peace happens through an encounter with those who are looked down on and marginalized in our society.

*

After having been part of anarchist and far-left American circles, Dorothy Day (1897–1980) discovered Jesus and the Catholic Church. Her heart burned for justice for all people. I met her in 1971. She started a community for street people in New York. This first house led to a hundred others throughout the United States. Dorothy Day lived among the most wounded people. Today, the Catholic Worker Movement continues this unconditional hospitality by serving the homeless, Latino immigrants caught in red tape, and others who are in precarious situations. Dorothy Day was also a passionate promoter of non-violence. She was a light for so many. She was not always looked on with favour by the Church, and was at times imprisoned for her anti–Vietnam war activism. But she never criticized the Church, as she was concerned with moving forward to herald a just social vision, a non-violent Jesus who was a friend of the poor.

*

I would also like to remember Sister Magdeleine Hutin (1898–1989). In 1921, through a book by René Bazin, she discovered the life of Charles de Foucauld, and decided to carry on his spiritual work. In 1939 she founded a new congregation, the Little Sisters of Jesus, which first spread to Algeria among nomadic Muslims, and then to many countries, always living in the poorest areas. I met her in Montreal's Lower Town, long before the foundation of L'Arche. Later, I saw Sister Magdeleine in Rome, at their General Fraternity. I am thankful to her for all these little fraternities hidden in the most difficult parts of the world, among those who suffered most, and the most marginalized. Later, I spent time with the Little Sisters in a Chicago ghetto. Imagine a cramped apartment on the fifth floor of a dilapidated building. A crucifix indicated the entrance, along with an image of the wounded heart of Jesus. I arrived during adoration of the Blessed Sacrament. What an offering… Lives offered to God, to help the marginalized. This same fraternity was the scene of tragedy that shocked me greatly. One day, a man from the neighbourhood drew a gun during a party, and shot a bullet into the air. The bullet came in the window, ricocheted through the room where the sisters were and hit one of them right in the heart – she who had given her life for the people of the ghetto. She died instantly. I met other Little Sisters in Europe, in Syria and in Muslim neighbourhoods in Palestine. Many of them shared our life, especially in Faith and Light communities. In Serbia, they were the ones who took me in. I was moved by their vision. Quietly, the Little Sisters throughout the world live their mission: being present to Jesus and being present to the poorest of the poor. Their fraternities are lights that brighten our wounded world.

40

The Power of Mercy

Allow me to share with you the text of a short video message that I loved – it's by Pope Francis and was posted online by the Vatican in January 2016 for the Year of Mercy. Francis says everything that needs to be said in 90 seconds. Speaking in Spanish, his mother tongue, the Pope calls people to pray that sincere dialogue between men and women of different religions may bear fruits of peace and justice.

"Most of the planet's inhabitants declare themselves believers. This should lead to dialogue among religions," he says. "We should not stop praying for it and collaborating with those who think differently." On the screen, we see several people representing different religious groups. All express their faith in their own words. "I have confidence in the Buddha," says Lama Rinchen Khandro; "I believe in God," says Rabbi Daniel Goldman; "I believe in Jesus Christ," proclaims Fr. Guillermo Marco; Islamic leader Omar Abboud says, "I believe in God, Allah."

Then the Pope says, "Many think differently, feel differently, seeking God or meeting God in different ways. In this crowd, in this range of religions, there is only one certainty we have for all: we are all children of God." Then, one after the other, the same faith leaders express a common belief: "I believe in love."

Yes, what unites us is greater than what divides us. This video moved me. Obviously, it raises all sorts of questions: What is love? But it is important. Why preach mercy? In his heart, the Pope longs to see divisions disappear between the healthy and the sick, between the rich and the poor, between people of different religions, different colours, often fuelled by fear. He is pained by the disunity that infects humanity, because even within the Church, we find deep divisions between those who push for strict observance of the law and those who want to reach out to all. He is pained because the mission of Jesus is to proclaim Good News to the poor. And he wants that message to get out. Mercy is not just going to confession, even though this sacrament offers us freedom to love better. Francis has this pain. He can't take these divisions anymore. And he tells us: go to the margins, go and encounter the outcast, as Jesus came to proclaim Good News to the poor. The pope has this cry: that humans will realize the enormous danger that faces them. If we don't wake up, we are heading for great peril. The big thing today, for all who believe, is this: to believe in your faith, learn to love. And love your enemy, as Jesus asked.

*

I admit that I am increasingly concerned when I see Christians inviting preachers or speakers to stir up a fear of Islam. We know that it doesn't take much for fear to turn to hatred. To me, these people go against the entire vision of Pope Francis, like that of John Paul II before him. Recall the gathering in Assisi in 1986, and the speech to Muslims of Morocco a year earlier. This vision is one of encounter, of friendship. A man like Bishop Pierre Claverie, killed in Oran, Algeria, in 1996, embodied this beautifully. So did Christian de Chergé and the monks of Tibhirine, also in Algeria. Yes, there are terrorists.

Yes, there are young people who have lost their way who profess allegiance to the so-called Islamic State. But we know that 80 percent of the victims of these extremists are Sunni and Shiite Muslims themselves, just as Yazidis and Christians are targeted because of their faith. These men who kill are not guided by a Muslim spirituality but by political ambition, the desire for power, a mad impulse for violence. I think it is urgent that we rediscover the spirit of Saint Francis of Assisi who, in 1219, guided by his small inner voice, left the crusaders' camp in Damiette to go and meet Sultan Al-Malik al-Kamil, with whom he stayed for several days. A mutual respect soon grew between them. The sultan was open to Francis, and Francis was open to the sultan. I would like to express here my friendship for all Muslims who are appalled by the terrorists and believe in the lenient and merciful God. Many of them long for democracy. During the recent Arab Spring, many yearned for peaceful resolutions, wanting to broaden basic freedoms, with a view to a more fraternal and humane world. I am not naive: I also know the seductive power of the strictest currents of Islam, but I still believe in a hope shared by many Muslims, who want to live their faith in peace in our societies.

Our Bethlehem community is for me a place of great joy. For the time being, only a day program is offered to these Palestinians with a disability who live with their parents. But it is a true community filled with joy and songs, while also being a workplace. Wool from Bethlehem sheep is made into adorable little sheep and miniature nativity scenes. The community is 80 percent Muslim and 20 percent Christian. There is undoubtedly love between them. In December 2015, a few weeks after the Paris attacks, I had a wonderful time with them. I can say that this fraternity that joins me to my Muslim brothers and sisters, assistants and people with an intellectual disability is a source of immense hope for me. When we go beyond our religious affiliations, we find that we are truly brothers and sisters, believers in a God of mercy.

The spiritual testament of Christian de Chergé, prior of the Trappist monastery of Tibhirine, written more than 20 years ago and left with his sister in case he was killed, remains for me topical. I like to meditate on these words, at a time when fear is building walls everywhere:

> For, God willing, I will be able to plunge my vision into the Father's in order to contemplate with Him His Islamic children just as He sees them, all illuminated with Christ's glory, fruits of His Passion, clothed by the gift of the Spirit whose secret joy will always be to establish communion and re-establish resemblance while enjoying the differences.

> I give thanks to God who seems to have wanted this lost life, completely mine and completely theirs, for heavenly JOY, for everything and despite everything.

> In this THANK YOU which says everything from now on about my life, I of course want to include you, friends of today and tomorrow, and you, friends here, beside my mother and father, my sisters and my brothers and their families, repaid a hundredfold as promised! And also to you, friend of the final hour, who will not know what you are doing.

> Yes, I also desire this THANK YOU for you, and this A-DIEU (TO-GOD) foreseen for you.

> May we be allowed to meet again as happy thieves in Paradise, if it pleases God, Father to both of us. AMEN!

41

An Encounter and a Risk

In 2016, Pope Francis called us to live a jubilee of mercy because he wanted, as he put it, "a Church that is poor and for the poor." For him, the poor have much to teach us. Earlier, he had said, "We need to let ourselves be evangelized by them. The new evangelization is an invitation to acknowledge the saving power at work in their lives…. We are called to find Christ in them, to lend our voice to their causes, but also to be their friends, to listen to them, to speak for them and to embrace the mysterious wisdom which God wishes to share with us through them" (*Evangelii gaudium*, no. 198). Mercy is an encounter and even a risk on the human level. Jesus, to show us who is our neighbour, describes a Samaritan who is filled with compassion for a Jew who is left beaten and bleeding (Luke 10:25-37). He encountered the man in an unexpected way. He took the risk of stopping to care for the injured man. He poured wine on his wounds to disinfect them, and oil to promote healing. Then he took care of him, watching over him for a whole night. The Jewish man's body was healed, but so was his spirit. He discovered the goodness of the Samaritan he had despised until then.

The Samaritan was also transformed. He began to love the Jewish man, and through him, the Jewish faith. Mercy is a risk. When I encounter someone who is poor, they awaken my heart.

Together we experience a moment of communion. I find that they are my fellow human, my brother or sister in humanity. And even if they do not share my religion or my culture, I don't know where they may lead me… They awaken the Holy Spirit in me. They bring me something new on the human level as well as grace. They awaken God in me.

This awakening, however, is sometimes painful. I remember a woman who accosted me in the city one day:

"Give me 10 euros."

"Why?"

"I'm hungry."

"Why are you hungry?

"I ran away from the psychiatric hospital."

I drew near to her to try to understand her situation, her needs. Then, suddenly, I was afraid. This woman would lead me too far if I stopped to listen to her. So I gave her 10 euros and went on my way. Mercy is an encounter. But it is a risk. I didn't want to go any farther that day; I didn't dare take the risk. We never know where the poor will lead us. Following Jesus is always a risk. But this risk is also a promise: Jesus will give us strength. Pope Francis's insistence on mercy must, it seems to me, be heard as a call to encounter people who are in great difficulty. To let them touch us. And, in the end, to experience communion. If we follow them, they may lead us where we are afraid to go, but this encounter will change our hearts, will make us more human, by opening us to the heart of God and a true experience of his kingdom. Being open to the poor and encountering them is always a grace given by the God of mercy, who transforms us and calls us to go farther.

Responding to the cry of the poor becomes a call. The call becomes an attraction. The attraction becomes generosity. Generosity becomes an encounter. The encounter becomes communion and the presence of God.

Mercy means moving downward. Towards the rejected, the broken, the marginalized. To lift them up and give them life. Moving downward also means looking at the Earth. At the beauty of our planet broken by greed: pollution of the water and the air, the destruction of living species... In his encyclical *Laudato si'*, Pope Francis warns us that taking care of our planet and saving human lives are two intertwined emergencies. There is an intimate connection between the terrible injustices of our societies and the environmental crisis. So many things are controlled by money. We work for ourselves, for the benefit of our small groups, forgetting our larger human family and the Earth we were given to share.

42

The Cry

I spoke earlier about Pauline, whom we welcomed at L'Arche. Her violence was a cry – a cry to be loved, to be known. A cry that breaks through walls. We know that God hears the cry of the poor. This is the cry of so many men and women who live a precarious existence in all the slums on the planet, in the deprived neighbourhoods of our cities. It is also the cry of all those who have been oppressed. This cry is like that of the newborn who emerges from its mother's body and whose lungs fill with air for the first time. It is the cry of anguish of the child wrested from the safety of its mother's womb to face an unknown world. This cry is at the beginning of all our lives. The cry can also be a call for help, when danger lurks. A cry that says: Come and help me. Not to mention the final cry of our lives. We often hide all these cries behind our gates and our masks, for we are afraid to reveal the depth of our heart. In each of us lies sleeping a cry to be loved. Unconditionally. And this cry brings us back to God's cry. The Anglican theologian David Ford, a friend of L'Arche whom I mentioned earlier, wrote that the kingdom of God is the cry of God meeting the cry of the poor. We know the cry of the poor; we hear it. We cannot ignore the clamour of all those who suffer, even if we sometimes hide so we can't hear them. But the cry of God is a mystery. Isn't this mystery revealed to us when Jesus speaks of the shepherd looking for the lost sheep? We don't hear anything about the joy of the sheep that is found. Rather, it is a question of the shepherd's joy (Luke 15). The shepherd's joy is that of God when he joins the cry of the poor who is lost. Yes, the Word was made flesh because of the cry of the poor. To share with us the Good News. The mystery of God lives in this immense yearning to give life. God is hurt when we refuse it. God yearns only for this joy. We hear the cry of God during the Jewish Festival of Tents, when Jesus gets up and exclaims, "Let anyone who is thirsty come to me, and let the one who believes in me drink" (John 7:37). This cry reveals Jesus' desire to live in communion with each one of us, and for each of us to be filled with everlasting joy. Jesus cries from the cross, "I am thirsty" (John 19:28). Saint Gregory, in his commentary on this passage, interprets it this way: "I thirst that they will thirst for me." God has a great desire to give life, to give joy, so that human beings do not remain imprisoned in tombs of death, sadness and fear. The heart of Jesus is a heart filled with love. He comes looking for us, if we leave some space for him. This is the meaning of the Greek term *parakletos* (the Paraclete), promised by Jesus (John 14), and which we can also translate as "the one who answers the call." The one who responds to the cry. This cry is made so that God comes and lives in our poverty. The cry springs from our poverty. And God is the one who responds to it. It is the God of humility who waits for the call. He respects our freedom so much that he will never enter by breaking in. "Listen! I am standing at the door, knocking; if you hear my voice and open the door, I will come in to you and eat with you, and you with me" (Revelation 3:20). God enters us when we let the deepest cry of our being flow and open the door of our hearts to him. God is Love. And our heart is thirsting for love. Yet, beyond the rocks that prevent our thirst from springing up and that block our hearts, what reigns, if not indifference? Yes, Love is not loved. Once we become humble and free, our hearts allow their thirst to overflow. The poor cry their thirst. The final words of the Bible are themselves a cry: the Spirit and the bride say, "Amen. Come, Lord Jesus" (Revelation 22:17). We must keep going downward, always. This need is not a gift or reward that God wants to give us. It is a communion. An encounter. A life.

43

Heaven's Ark

Some time ago, Marie-Jo died. Years earlier, we had welcomed her to La Forestière, one of our specialized homes in Trosly. She was part of L'Arche for so long. It is always a painful time in the community when one of our members leaves us. Especially when it is sudden. Marie-Jo went into cardiac arrest. We got her to the hospital, but it was too late. She died on the way.

Death... It is an appointment that awaits us all. When a death happens in the community, we have the habit of gathering the night before the funeral. This is what we did for Marie-Jo. Together, we shared our memories and photos of her. We remembered her life, especially the cries she uttered sometimes in a bout of suffering. Unable to speak, Marie-Jo had a particular cry. A cry that said: I am hurting. Or: I feel all alone. Sometimes it was a cry of joy, of exuberance. Often, it was a way of saying: I exist, I am here! Don't forget me! Now here we were gathered around her. Each of us had a history with Marie-Jo. We cried. We laughed. And we didn't forget to sing, because for us, death is also a time to give thanks. Yes, thank you, Jesus, for sending us Marie-Jo. She was so beautiful and so poor in her wheelchair. Thank you, because in living with us, she changed so many assistants. Those who knew Marie-Jo were often deeply shaken, transformed. Because with Marie-Jo, as with Éric and all the others, you must take time. Time to enter into communion. Time to be with them. Time to experience a presence. Thank you, Marie-Jo...

The next day, after mass, we carried her to the earth. Again, the whole community stood together. United in this great act of thanksgiving, a song of praise arose from our hearts. Among the large numbers who have been members of L'Arche communities during the more than 50 years of our existence, we have had countless deaths. Death is an important moment when we send to Jesus the one who shows us a way to him. A moment of great joy and profound thanksgiving. Then comes the final leave-taking. The last goodbye. Everyone goes forward to place a little flower on the casket, after blessing it by sprinkling it with a little water. Goodbye, Marie-Jo; you will always be there to watch over us. We need you more than ever; you are now in Heaven's ark.

Heaven's ark: a huge family in God of men and women who have been marginalized, now reunited in extraordinary unity and joy, with those who walked with them on earth. I think of three of them, Jacqueline, Barbara and Claire, from the beginnings of L'Arche, who sowed joy through their love, their laughter, their smile and the gift of themselves.

44

Walking in Weakness

I gradually gave up my responsibilities at L'Arche, starting with my own community in 1980. Then, at age 75, taking advantage of a meeting of our coordinators from around the world, I asked to leave the international council. I will no longer be involved in the organic operation of L'Arche, but I can keep giving retreats and talks when I am invited. I saw this surrendering as a real liberation. I was removed from the daily problems. I could – and must – place all my trust in L'Arche's structures and leaders. I was free to continue living with the people I shared a home with. Free to live with God. In my community, I still had to struggle with my human challenges, especially when it came to relationships: I was somewhat surprised to show my knowledge without acting superior. I was well aware that I needed more than ever to disarm myself, to become more humble, to make more room for others. In short, to become more free. It is a constant battle. Frankly, I had to embrace my compulsions and know that behind them remained many secret anxieties that left me powerless. In this book, I have mentioned moments of joy but also of suffering that affected me greatly, especially regarding the sexual relations that Fr. Thomas had with several women, who were deeply scarred and wounded by this abuse.

✳

My whole life, I have also had to struggle with myself: I have spent a large part of my life with wounded people, but also with my own weaknesses and poverty. I have my own sensibilities and my own needs to love and be loved. I am a person like everyone else, who can feel empathy for some, and can also avoid others. I may therefore have hurt others. At the end of this book and the end of my life, I would like to ask their forgiveness from the bottom of my heart. In Calcutta, during the last general meeting of L'Arche that I attended, in the face of such beauty coming from L'Arche, beauty that amazed me so much, I felt the need to ask forgiveness for all my weaknesses and mistakes. Once again, in the evening of my life, I am asking forgiveness. Sometimes, I was oppressed by my own weaknesses. Yes, I can see pride in me when I look at my life and have trouble fully accepting my mistakes, my faults. I believe in the mercy of God who led so many events in the history of L'Arche through my weaknesses. I thank God for his faithfulness, for my poverty did not prevent his work from being accomplished. I realize more and more that L'Arche, in its development and in the deepening of its spirituality, sprang from the mercy of God that chose the weak and the foolish to carry out his plan.

What is life like for the 89-year-old man that I am now? In the little house where I live, near the chapel and La Ferme in Trosly, my joy is to proclaim Jesus, to proclaim the foolishness and demands of the Gospel during the retreats I lead at La Ferme. Proclaiming life with the marginalized of our societies as a way of peace. And each day, this joy culminates during the meals I am able to share at my home – Val fleuri – with Pat, Annicette, David, Michel, André ("Doudoul") and all my other friends. I think also of Odile Ceyrac, whom I mentioned earlier, to whom L'Arche entrusted the mission of keeping an eye on my health and my advanced age.

I am definitely older than I was in 1964. But today, just like on the first day of L'Arche, I can recapture the uncontrollable laughter, the freedom to be a little silly and the times of silence experienced together in prayer. The heart of our community is the foolishness of believing that love is possible, and that to live with the marginalized is to live with Jesus. It is also the hope for utopia.

My desire, in growing old, is to live what I have always proclaimed: that God is at the heart of weakness. "My grace is sufficient for you, for power is made perfect in weakness," Jesus says to Paul (2 Corinthians 12:9). I would like, in my old age, with the possible loss of memory, mobility and even speech, to keep proclaiming this presence. At the end of this path, I must descend to the ultimate weakness with great thanksgiving to God for all he has given me.

45

The Joy of a Presence

Jesus said that anyone who welcomes a little child in his name welcomes him and the one who welcomes Jesus welcomes the Father. There is something extraordinary in welcoming Jesus like a child. To play with him, to be happy with him. The Gospel says several times that Jesus ate with tax collectors and sinners. I think he experienced joy with them. I'm not sure that everything he said was serious. A meal is a place for friendship, a time of celebration. And that is what we have found at L'Arche. Jesus tells us that we are blessed or happy when we invite the poor, the lame and the blind to our table. Eating together means entering into friendship. It's revealing to the other person their value: a time of communion. Isn't this the heart of L'Arche? Being happy together, eating together, celebrating together?

Sometimes I lie on my bed and try to spend time with Jesus. And I laugh, though I am the only one there. I'm a bit like Patrick, and I think I can say I am happy. Yes, my happiness is obvious: I feel loved. I am happy because Jesus is Jesus. I like to thank him for what he is and what he gives us. Being with him, in silence or in laughter. Isn't being in communion with him delighting in a presence?

I feel particularly called to pray for those who are suffering. I also pray for all those who cause this suffering: criminals, terrorists and all those who do not acknowledge the weak. So they can have an experience of Jesus, knowing the joy of being loved by God and having their heart changed as God changed mine. As I have just said, I find at L'Arche another aspect of the presence of Jesus: being happy with him, thanking him for who he is, resting in him. I am in awe of the littleness of Jesus, of his humility. The way he has of hiding, when he can do any-thing. He chooses to bury his omnipotence in the weakness of a child. A little child who wants to play, a little child who needs to be loved, a little child who just wants to rest, a little child who lives in the Father's heart. I still have a long way to go to develop this gift from God: this gracious and joyful presence with Jesus, the place of my joy.

46

At the End of the Road...
A Time of Waiting and a Promise

The history of humanity, since its beginning, is as if hidden in a thick cloud. In this cloud violence prevailed, carried on from generation to generation. God intervened quietly in our history to transform this violence by showing us a path of peace: God himself became flesh. He became a human being, in all its fragility, to show us a way that goes through weakness and humility. Jesus is very different from the idea the Jewish people had about the Messiah. He did miracles, yes. But above all he came to live among the poorest and the weakest, to become a friend of the marginalized. He welcomed sinners, prostitutes and tax collectors at his table. Jesus came to reveal that the kingdom of God is intertwined with the world of the marginalized. But the people didn't want to listen. The religious authorities clung to a legal religion that followed the rules, enclosed within its certainties, with all requirements originating in the Law. A religion of power, I would even say, at least for those who placed burdens on others (Matthew 23). Jesus came to reveal something different. The poor are a presence of God. He stayed the course and we rejected him. We didn't want him. We put him to death. How can we forget his final cry, the cry of a poor person: "Father, forgive them, for they do not know what they are doing" (Luke 23:34). We now live in the time between Jesus' cry on the cross and the final words of the Bible, in the Revelation to John: "Come, Lord Jesus!"

We are in a time of waiting, which is also a promise.

Come, Lord Jesus, for we can no longer bear it. We are tired of suffering. We are tired of divisions. We are tired of seeing our beautiful garden – the Earth – ransacked by the greed of nations and those with power. And Jesus lets us know: he will come. But he will come in the hearts of the poor and the marginalized. As Fr. Joseph Wresinski says, the marginalized are our saviours. People with a disability show us the way to the kingdom. The cry of the poor springs from our humanity at war, where so much hatred, contempt and desire for power remain. The cry of Jesus is the cry of a poor person: "Let anyone who is thirsty come to me, and let the one who believes in me drink" (John 7:37). Jesus is like a lover who wants to draw each person to himself. Jesus knocks on the door of our hearts. He waits for us to say yes so he can come in and eat at our table. To become our friend. Yes, come, Lord Jesus, come…

But he is already there, hidden in the poor. In the faces of people with a disability, on the lips of children screaming their distress, in the hearts of people with mental illness, those living with addiction or dementia. He comes, hidden deep within the marginalized. He is there, burning to enter into relationship with us. This final cry, "Come, Lord Jesus," is a call to look at those on the other side of the wall, on the other side of the road that no one dares to cross. A call to encounter. To encounter the other, especially the poor, those who are hungry and thirsty, the prisoner, the refugee, the migrant, the naked, the one who is crying for help. For it is through this encounter that our heart will open and the spring of living water will flow. To those who draw near to the marginalized to give bread and water, and a gesture of love and fellowship, Jesus says: "Come, you that are blessed by my Father, inherit the kingdom prepared for you from the foundation of the world" (Matthew 25:34). This is the cry of the poor: Come! Those who listen discover a presence of Jesus.

From a Lord God, a God of power, master and king, my path gradually led me to encounter Jesus who comes to wash our feet. Jesus, hidden in the weak and the small. Welcoming vulnerability reveals his presence. A prayer of hope rises to my lips:

Blessed are you, Father,
Master and Lord of the world, to have hidden these things from the wise and the knowledgeable,
and revealed them to the littlest ones.
Blessed are you for your Spirit, whereby the littlest ones and the oppressed
become the face of Jesus. Together,
let us learn to pass through walls and checkpoints,
let us learn to cross the roads that separate rich from poor so we can become messengers of peace. Together,
let us learn to encounter each other in compassion,
in goodness, in humility,
and let us know how to discover
through welcoming the oppressed
the communion between people, a fellowship that thus becomes communion with Jesus,
and in him with the Father. In this way we wish to prepare your coming:
Come, Lord Jesus, come! Amen.